Praise

'*Leading on the Edge* is a call to your soul. It challenges you to ask a most fundamental question, one that has guided me most of my life, "What must I be about in this life, to live the life I came here to live, and not someone else's life?" This book is about saying yes to how life wants to live you. It is about the boldness, courage and audacity required to live and lead at the edge of this most fundamental question. It asks you to wake up to how you are aching to serve and get about it—come what may. There is no safe way to do this. It requires leading at the edge. That's the deal.'

   — **Bob Anderson**, Founder Leadership
      Circle, Co-Author *Mastering Leadership*
      and Scaling Leadership

'*Leading on the Edge* goes beyond leadership theory. It is a call to action for those who dare to lead with purpose and conviction. Zana's insights remind us that true leadership is about creating a legacy by embracing uncertainty and inspiring those around us to do the same. This book challenges us to think differently, to engage meaningfully and to leave a positive impact on the world. With *Leading on the Edge*, Zana does what she does best, she inspires us to lead and live with Boldness.'

   — **Bruno Casadinho**, Managing Director and
      Executive Vice President at Capgemini
      Engineering Asia Pacific and Middle East

'*Leading on the Edge* is a transformative guide that asks provocative questions, challenges conventional leadership paradigms and inspires bold action. As a former Partner at PwC and now a leadership coach, I appreciate the book's compelling blend of personal narrative and actionable insights through reflective Mirroring Moments, urging leaders to get real, to care and to embrace discomfort as a catalyst for growth.

'Zana Goic Petricevic's powerful message of claiming one's arena and start leading on the edge resonates deeply, making this a must-read for anyone committed to meaningful change.'

— **Günter Westphal**, CEO of Moving Mountains and former PwC Senior Partner

'*Leading on the Edge* is a masterclass in what it means to embrace the uncomfortable truth of our time: growth, resilience and bold leadership are born where safety ends. Zana Goic Petricevic challenges us to rethink our relationship with fear, inviting us to sit with its discomfort long enough to find strength and possibility.

'Her work resonates deeply with the human experience, weaving together neuroscience, emotional intelligence and real-life reflections. Zana reminds us that leadership is not reserved for the extraordinary – it is for those brave enough to be fully human, to fail, to learn, and to lead forward anyway.

'This book does more than inspire; it sparks the realisation that we are already equipped to create change, in ways both small and seismic. It's an essential companion for anyone daring to step into their purpose.'
— **Mirjam Johansson**, Leadership Coach, Organisational Consultant and CEO of DevelUpment AB

'If you need someone to hold up the mirror, ask soul-searching questions, hold your hand and heart with compassion, offer understanding and give you permission to be YOU—capital letters, bold and brave—the kind of YOU that fills you with pride, then take this book, immerse yourself and let *Leading on the Edge* lead you to those places.'
— **Ana Gongola**, Sandoz/Country Head Croatia and Slovenia Commercial Operations

'This book serves as both an inspiration and a guide for making meaningful contributions while fostering personal growth. Initially, it advocates for living with passion, courage and authenticity, encouraging readers to lead boldly in areas they care about deeply. Subsequently, it provides a clear and concrete roadmap to achieve these goals. The content is both pragmatic and uplifting, offering advice derived from practical experience and supported by numerous case studies.'
— **Shail Jain**, CEO, FARRAGUT

'In a world where disruption and uncertainty are the new normal, we face a choice: accept the status quo or take action. If you're among the few who choose to step forward, you have the opportunity to achieve something truly transformative for yourself and others. Having worked with Zana on this book and her first, I've seen firsthand how she truly walks her talk. Her insights and experience shine through in *Leading on the Edge*, offering space for reflection, tools for exploration and practical guidance to help you live and lead boldly, leaving doubt and fear behind.'

— **Karen Williams**, The Book Mentor, Librotas

ZANA GOIC
PETRICEVIC

LEADING ON THE EDGE

The bold art of being more
irrational and less mediocre

R^ethink

First published in Great Britain in 2025
by Rethink Press (www.rethinkpress.com)

Cover image © Shutterstock | inamar

Illustrations © Mario Pereda Dominguez 2024

To my son Noa

Choose boldly, reject mediocrity—let the world benefit from your resounding 'hell yes'.

Contents

Foreword

*L*eading on the Edge challenges us to confront the uncomfortable realities of our time, showing that growth, resilience and effective leadership arise at the peripheries of safety.

I've learnt firsthand that great leadership isn't about sitting behind a desk. Effective leadership requires a proactive stance, enabling leaders to discern insights that may not be readily visible.

Leading from the forefront has consistently been a pivotal element in my tenure at the Homeless World Cup Foundation, as well as in my extensive involvement with various initiatives and organisations. This entails engaging with our events, visiting teams or beneficiaries of our efforts and participating in a multitude of activities, thereby cultivating a more profound understanding of our actual circumstances, particularly regarding the significance of the Homeless World Cup Foundation and our annual event, the Homeless World Cup.

These on-the-ground experiences have shown me time and again that being present reveals truths no spreadsheet or report ever could. When you witness firsthand the impact of your work, you gain insights that transform how you think about leadership.

Zana Goic Petricevic gets it. She advocates for leaders to embrace fear, urging an exploration of its discomfort to reveal a leader's true strength and potential. She challenges us to face our fears head-on, showing how leaning into discomfort reveals our genuine strength and potential. Reading her insights, I found myself nodding along, recognising numerous professional and personal experiences from my career, integrating principles from a vast array of experiences, positive and negative.

Yes, sometimes we need the bird's-eye view of strategy. But there's irreplaceable value in rolling up your sleeves and experiencing challenges firsthand. Zana's insights in her book have reinforced my conviction that to comprehend the challenges encountered across any part of an organisation however small, leaders must observe and embrace them directly. The conversations you have on the ground—whether with team members or those your organisation serves—bring perspectives that transform how you lead and the decisions you make.

What I love most about this book is Zana's powerful reminder: leadership is not reserved for the exceptional; it is attainable for those willing to embrace their humanity, to confront failure, to learn and to persevere.

Leading on the Edge not only serves as an inspiration but also ignites the understanding that we possess the capability to effect change, whether in modest or significant manners. It is an essential resource for anyone dedicated to pursuing their purpose.

Mel Young, President and Co-Founder, Homeless World Cup Foundation

Call To Arms

This book is born out of two – arguably connected – realisations. The first is captured in a sobering statement often attributed to Benjamin Franklin that suggests many people are effectively dead by the time they reach twenty-five but aren't buried until they reach seventy-five. It's a thought-provoking concept that immediately struck me with the uncomfortable truth it holds: are the fifty years in between truly worth living this way?

While this message is sobering, it also highlights a paradox, which led me to my second realisation. In a world where so much feels absurd and nonsensical, what we truly lack are those brilliantly irrational ideas – the kind so bold they defy conventional logic. These ideas call on us to abandon the comfortable, predictable and safe paths, urging us to take risks in the pursuit of creating something truly extraordinary. Yet, as humans, we are often reluctant to embrace risk, and so we settle. The result is a prevalence of mediocrity in the way we live and lead.

Before we speak of the bold, irrational ideas, let me share what I mean by a world that often feels absurd and nonsensical. I'm alluding to the paradox of our global home, our world that is both inspiring and discouraging at the same time. I'm thinking of our workplace that is, even though it's intended to be a space where we engage and realise our full potential, deeply flawed, often shutting us down instead of allowing us to flourish. I'm pointing to our immediate surroundings, the landscape in which we operate on a day-to-day basis, encountering numerous situations, unwritten rules and experiences that do not serve us, and yet we still normalise them instead of daring to question them.

There are countless things that could be transformed into something that would make so much more sense if only we dared to challenge the way they are and believe in our ideas of change, even if, when they first appear, these ideas may momentarily seem so much bigger than us. Instead, we hold back, simply because no one has done it before. Even when we care very much about our ideas, we give up before we try.

Within each of us, there are numerous innate skills that could support us in creating a real change every step of our way, but they remain unused. We tend to rationalise what, in truth, goes against the very essence of our human needs and nature. All that all too often makes little sense.

That nonsense is our greatest challenge today. In their article 'Fourth person',[1] researchers Otto Scharmer and Eva Pomeroy discuss the key issue of our time. They say it's not climate change, inequality, artificial intelligence (AI) or war. Instead, humanity's greatest challenge is our belief in our lack of agency to address these problems. In other words, we are perfectly capable, but unready to dare.

Let me clarify what I mean by agency in this context. It is our responsibility as leaders to create what we care about most in our environment. It is also within our power to shape a better world through more decisive, bolder leadership, so how do we recognise our agency within ourselves?

It manifests as a compelling inner voice urging us to act and not just observe. It is the conviction that we can answer this call and effect real change. Agency is intertwined with our sense of self and autonomy, fuelling our feeling of ownership over our decisions and supporting our belief in our influence.

Our environment more often than not seeks to erode our sense of agency, making us feel too fearful to initiate the changes we desire. Our agency begins in our belief that we've got it. Equally, it is extinguished in the exact same place – our belief that we don't have it. This paradox explains how we can be simultaneously capable and reluctant; fully equipped yet remaining hesitant to act boldly.

We must challenge the mindset that tries to convince us we lack agency. This book is designed to provide the activational inspiration needed to do precisely that.

Each of us is inherently bold – that is a fundamental truth. There is no divide between those who are born with boldness and those who seemingly are not; there is no exclusive circle of bold leaders that only a few who 'get it' can enter. We are all bold. Denying this truth is the first step towards sabotaging our potential to lead on the edge.

While we are naturally bold, we are also rarely convinced of that before we dare to act. That's why there comes a moment when it's crucial to go beyond mere self-discovery. While we dive into deeper layers of our inner selves, we must also take deliberate actions in the external world.

This is essentially what this book is about – your decision to put your innate boldness into action even before you feel ready. It's high time you responded to the call of your agency and activated your boldness.

It's also true that not all of us will trust ourselves enough to activate our boldness. In an inspiring commencement speech at Dartmouth College in June 2024, Roger Federer, the legendary tennis player widely regarded as one of the greatest athletes of all time, said that trusting yourself is a talent.[2] While some people are born with it, he added, everyone must work at it.

I'm not convinced that only some are born with the great quality of trusting themselves. I believe we are all born with it, and it's something we must continue to nurture and develop throughout our lives. For me, this isn't about belonging to an elite group immune to self-doubt. Self-doubt and uncertainty are universal; whether they are fleeting or prolonged, they arise for everyone. The real question is how long we choose to remain in those moments.

Some leaders may see trusting themselves as a pressure, which could explain why they find a long-term comfort in self-doubt. Self-doubt can provide a safe escape from one's own agency. In contrast, once you trust yourself, you realise that no one else is coming to save you. Instead, you acknowledge that you are fully capable of saving yourself and achieving so much more. It's the moment when you become ready to dare.

For those asking how you can do that, I'm afraid the answer is less sophisticated than you might expect – you just do it. It's a matter of decision.

Whether you're ready to make that decision, getting close or just curious, this book aims to help you realise that leading on the edge means tapping into extraordinary possibilities in every circumstance, making sense of every turn during those fifty (or more or fewer) years in between.

Why not you, why not now?

You don't want to wait half a century to be buried, do you? I know I don't. Theoretically, I might not even have half a century left, but I know that I don't want to wait even a year. I refuse to be a dead woman walking. I want to feel truly alive, making every step count in this pivotal moment in history. I want to be present with purpose, taking action that creates real change, leaving the world better than I found it. I want to honour the true essence of leadership – changing the present into a better future.

To convey a sense of urgency, there's an exercise I often use with the leaders I coach. It involves visualising their lifespan up to ninety years, marking their current age and contemplating what they wish to achieve with the time they have remaining. This perspective sharpens their focus on the hunger within them, the change they dare to articulate and the risks they are willing to take to make that change a reality. It confirms their conviction, no matter how scary it sounds, that the future is indeed shaped by their actions.

While preparing a session for one of my clients and their top 10% of talented leaders, I initiated a conversation about this exact task of ours – actively shaping the future. A leader from that organisation offered a profound reminder of our true leadership work: 'The future is not a destination. It's a canvas awaiting our brushstrokes and every action we take is a stroke that paints the masterpiece of the future of our community, our organisation, our life, our children, our world.'

A leader is an artist – an expert in the art of boldness with a unique masterpiece inside them, unlike any other. Gordon MacKenzie, author of *Orbiting the Giant Hairball* in which he speaks about creativity being crucial to business success, warns us that if we go to our grave without painting our masterpiece, it will not get painted: 'No one else can paint it. Only you.'[3]

Why would you hesitate? Why not you? Why not now?

I want to lead. Do you want to lead? If you do, you're needed – now more than ever.

If you're content with just holding a leadership role and being labelled a 'leader' within the system, here's the uncomfortable truth: that is vastly different from truly leading. I challenge you – what are you willing to risk as a leader and for what purpose? Our world is yearning for purposeful leaders – those individuals willing to replace patterns of self-preservation with bold leadership, shaping a world that looks and feels far more extraordinary for all of us.

I'm not interested in your job title. I'm interested in the change you're hungry for – and you should be too. If you're not, if nothing about your context concerns you, if there's no change you want to bring to your leadership landscape for the greater good in service of others, then please step down. If you're not stepping down, then refuse to stand in mediocrity.

It's time to take action: learn, trust, risk and change. Embark on your quest. Get clear, get ready and step into the spotlight with your bold, even if irrational, ideas. More importantly, bring others with you – create partnerships, spark movements.

Risk, risk and risk again. Finish what you start, celebrate your wins and move on to your next project, your next mission, your next walk on the edge. Keep pushing for change. Keep the conversation alive, no matter where you lead. The time is now. The leader is you. Begin.

Introduction

At every opportunity, I passionately communicate this message to the leaders I work with: 'Enough of playing around – the world needs you.' My intention is to empower them to transform their leadership and, in turn, their world – whether within their organisation or in any other setting.

The world is changing faster than ever, and as leaders, we must rise to meet the moment. This requires a profound shift in mindset and a transformation in how we think, act and lead. Leadership is not about maintaining the status quo; it is about outpacing who we are today and setting the stage for our next-level selves to emerge bolder than ever before.

Too often, leaders remain stuck in mediocrity, hesitant to act boldly in ways that could transform themselves and their surroundings. This book is a call to action for those ready to make a different choice – one that elevates them beyond mediocrity to step out of their comfort zones and lead on the edge of possibility.

This book is for leaders – formal or informal, organisational or personal – who feel the urge to create something extraordinary in their context. Whether you're leading a team, an organisation or simply yourself, *Leading on the Edge* invites you to embrace boldness, reject mediocrity and activate your full leadership potential.

The promise of this book is both straightforward and transformative: through its content, you will gain the mindset, tools and inspiration to lead boldly within your unique landscape for change. Most importantly, you will rediscover and strengthen your sense of agency – your power and responsibility to create what matters most to you in your leadership landscape, even when it challenges convention and requires the courage to walk along the risky edge beyond mediocrity.

Why this book?

Mediocre leadership is distressingly common and has a detrimental effect on all of us. It is a frustrating waste of boldness potential. Over the years, I've witnessed far too much mediocre leadership that leaves bold-ness untapped in organisations. Organisations have immense potential to create meaningful change, but that potential remains locked away unless leaders dare to act boldly.

Unlocking that potential starts with a simple yet pro-found question that no leader can avoid: *What are you willing to risk as a leader, and for the sake of what?*

Having heard many leaders' stories, I've realised that they all experience one common challenge: leading change in their leadership landscape – their closest day-to-day reality. When it comes to change, they need to know what they are ready to risk and what for. If they are not truly ready to risk anything in their comfortable world, they must question why anyone would want to be led by them.

Unfortunately, many leaders avoid both the risk and the change, even though paradoxically, doing so lim-its their potential and prevents them from achieving outcomes they deeply care about. They could make a significant impact if only they were willing to act boldly – even if it meant being labelled as irrational. Instead, they choose the safe, familiar path and fail to make a real difference.

When leaders stay mediocre, it becomes a collec-tive crisis – a crisis this book is designed to address. Mediocre leaders abandon their agency. They miss the chance to shape a better world through their leadership, leaving behind a story that concludes: 'We could have done so much, but we did nothing.'

Leaders, where is this closing line taking you – and everyone else? We are not powerless. This book challenges mediocrity and introduces leading on the edge as a mindset that reveals bold possibilities.

To truly understand this mindset, you'll find powerful stories in this book of individuals who are anything but mediocre. They are real and their work is bold – just as your work can be. Their stories originate from diverse contexts and aim to inspire you to rise beyond mediocrity and lead on the edge. The cost of your hesitant leadership is simply too high, whatever context you lead in.

How this book works

Leading on the Edge is divided into three parts, each designed to guide you through a thought-provoking and eventually transformational process.

World on the Edge. This section examines the context in which we lead through three different lenses, each one coming progressively closer to our day-to-day reality: global, organisational and personal. It invites you to see your leadership landscape – your closest context for creating change.

Leadership on the Edge. Here, the focus shifts inward, exploring the 'being' aspects of leadership, reminding you that leading begins with your ways of being. You'll learn to confront your limiting beliefs and cultivate the boldness needed to lead on the edge. The being part is a request to develop a bold mindset, a bold view on leadership, as a foundation for bold action.

Daring on the Edge. This final section emphasises action. You'll discover how to turn bold ideas into impactful change, drawing on real-world examples of leaders who've succeeded in transforming their contexts. This 'doing' aspect of leadership is a reminder that bold leaders are truly bold only when they dare to take risky actions that go beyond mediocrity. It's at this point that they lead on the edge of real change.

Each section aims to refine your understanding: the context clarifies the arena in which you intend to create change; the being challenges your mindset to support that intention; and the doing offers a roadmap with clear actions you need to take to make a real difference.

At the end of each chapter, you'll find **your mirror moment** with thought-provoking questions. At the end of each part, **your activation zone** challenges you to identify and implement game-changing ideas in your unique landscape for change. These exercises are designed to bridge the gap between inspiration and action, ensuring this book is as practical as it is inspirational.

Why me?

I know the risk of choosing boldness first hand. My journey has been shaped by moments of profound challenge and transformation. If you've read my book *Bold Reinvented*,[4] you may already know my story. In 2011, I was removed from my corporate role after nearly a decade of service – physically kicked out by my chairman from the head office. That moment marked the death of one identity. For years, I resisted burying it, blind to the possibility of creating something remarkable from that transformational experience.

When I finally let go, a bolder self began to emerge. With this new self, I walked on the edge, challenging power structures, reshaping my leadership and building a bold leadership business that has allowed me to work with extraordinary clients across the globe.

This unpleasant event triggered a series of long court cases in the Croatian justice system, lasting thirteen years at the time of writing. Taking on a major organisation in court for over a decade is a daunting task anywhere, but in Croatia, it demands a unique blend of perseverance, patience and a touch of irrationality. For much of this time, I longed for the cases to end so I could live freely, but a relentless inner voice urged me to trust the process and keep walking this edge, one step at a time.

This voice steered me away from courtroom distractions and towards a realisation: the edge offered an opportunity to lead boldly in my own leadership landscape – my daily reality. Letting go of my need for comfort, I embraced the seemingly irrational idea of challenging conventional understandings of power and proving we are not powerless against oppression. For thirteen years, I've faced countless obstacles while discovering vast possibilities on this edge.

This shift began with a simple mindset change. Instead of asking, 'When will this end?' I wondered, 'What if this is an invitation for...?' Rather than feeling powerless over what others might see as something 'happening to me', I chose to lead this risky experience and build my bold leadership business upon it.

Walking on this edge has revealed my deepest passions and my fundamental choices in life. I became strong and ready to confront what felt wrong, even when it seemed utterly irrational to others. This journey has been about risking many things so I would not risk the most precious one – my integrity. Along the way, I've witnessed profound change in myself, the people I impact through my work and the contexts in which I lead.

Some say I've already achieved enough and should abandon this uncomfortable path, but they fail to see the direct link between my leadership inspiration and walking on this edge. I remain committed to uncovering even more boldness. My story is not one of comfort but of continuous transformation. It's this lived experience that empowers me to guide you through the thrill and benefit of leading on the edge.

When we lead on the edge, we are invincible and the world gains the most. When we hesitate, our leadership becomes mediocre and our world meaningless. This book aims to inspire those who hesitate so that bold, seemingly irrational ideas can flourish, making our world meaningful and our leadership extraordinary.

This book isn't about me – it's about you. Your context, your challenges and your potential to create extraordinary change. All that matters is your willingness to act boldly, step into your agency and inspire others to join you.

Are you ready to begin?

This book is an invitation to embrace the true task of leadership: change the present into a better future by disrupting many things that we normalise for the sake of creating a new and improved world. It is a call to action for those ready to reject mediocrity and act in service of something greater.

Given my work in organisational settings, I am eager to see this book resonate with many organisational leaders. I struggle to accept that such significant engines of financial wealth and nurseries of human potential are not filled with many more bold ideas we need to make this world a better place.

Ultimately, this book is for anyone who dares to imagine a better future and is willing to take the risks necessary to create it. It's for anyone ready to fall in love with never-ending change, no matter how uncomfortable, seeing it as a walk on the edge of possibilities. It is for all those individuals who, regardless of their context, are willing to risk their own significance and take bold leadership action in a world that grows better through continuous, often scary, transformation.

If that sounds like you, then you're in the right place. Let's begin the journey.

WORLD

WORKPLACE

LANDSCAPE FOR CHANGE

PART 1
WORLD ON THE EDGE

'No one wants to destroy the world,' declares Sam Altman, CEO of OpenAI, as he discusses what he calls the 'existential risk' surrounding AI.[5] Altman was featured as one of the top thinkers in the January/February 2024 issue of *Prospect Magazine*, a renowned UK publication that annually brings together a list of individuals making a significant impact through their ideas and actions in climate, economics, freedom, geopolitics and technology.

With the launch of OpenAI's humanly intelligent chatbot ChatGPT in November 2022, Altman went beyond the tech world as ChatGPT quickly became the fastest-growing consumer app of all time, driving him into the public eye. *Prospect Magazine* describes him as 'more of an investor and entrepreneur than a scientific genius', noting that his thinking and leadership 'for good or ill' are driving both the progress of AI and the global discussion around it.[6] Whether for better or worse, the impact of AI will most likely be on the edge of both good and bad.

Though it's not easy to either say or accept, we must face the reality that the entire world is on the edge of dark and light. Instability and crises in global affairs, environmental concerns, political tensions, economic uncertainty and social unrest alongside technological advancements, breakthroughs in healthcare, innovations in renewable energy and greater global connectivity – these are just a few of the factors affecting us for both good and bad.

Prospect Magazine introduces the views of its top thinkers with a grounding perspective: 'As a planet and a civilisation, we are approaching tipping points – some frightening, others freeing – that will transform life as we know it.'[7] One of the important questions is, what does this mean for us as leaders?

We could so easily succumb to the impact the teetering world has on us, which can be anything from overwhelm to overdrive; we might find ourselves retreating into passivity or distance, or jumping overly readily into rescuer action. As humans, we all react differently.

That said, it's important to give ourselves permission to normalise our reactions to the impact the world on the edge has on us, and here's why. In a context where the circumstances seem intense, allowing ourselves to be affected with no judgement over our reactions opens up space for us to see these challenges as an invitation to lead.

This is really about holding a tension between embracing our humanity and owning our responsibility as leaders. In holding that tension, we ensure every situation presents an opportunity to make a difference – especially if we're ready to risk. Possibilities exist across the entire landscape in which we lead, and we can spot them almost anywhere if we look for them. I understand that this may sound simple, yet I also know that it is incredibly challenging to embrace when we are affected by a world on the edge.

What does it really mean to be affected by a world on the edge?

While we may feel that we operate solely within our personal leadership environment – our day-to-day circle of impact – that's just one piece of a larger puzzle. Looking at this larger puzzle, I see it consists of three interconnected lenses or perspectives that shape the overall context in which we lead. These perspectives provide us with a real opportunity to bring bold leadership to life in our immediate environment, which will eventually extend the impact even further.

Let's briefly look at what each of these lenses reveals. We will explore this in more detail in the coming chapters:

1. **World as our global home.** This is the broadest lens, encompassing the wider context in which we live, including economic, social, political, environmental and many other factors. We continuously feel the impact of these factors in our closest world, more than we realise.

2. **Workplace as our microworld.** Given that we spend most of our awake time at work, our workplaces essentially become our world. They are a significant part of our daily lives, affected by both disruptions and our often broken approach towards them. Our workplaces are shaping what we believe to be possible or impossible in our closest reality more than we would like.

3. **Landscape for change as our personal leadership environment.** This is the leadership landscape we engage with every day: our most immediate reality, where the previous two perspectives – world events and workplace trends – intersect, often amplifying the challenges we face. In addition, this landscape reflects our personal stories and experiences of navigating our own world on the edge – how external pressures and internal struggles shape our leadership actions. I call it our landscape for change because it represents the closest context where potential for change and our own potential can be realised. In these spaces, it becomes impossible to hide the one thing that ultimately defines us as leaders: our agency.

Each of these lenses affects us and can push us to the edge. In the last one, which is closest and most real to us, we face two choices: remain waiting at the edge, focusing on our sense of safety and security, or start walking on the edge, transforming it into our ally, together with its accompanying discomfort. Once an ally, it communicates to us the critical change we passionately care about. It clarifies for us our fundamental choice that helps us in claiming our arena and bringing our agency – our boldness – into action to create the change we wish to see.

The world, the workplace and your landscape – all these three interconnected lenses are inviting you to show up and ask yourself: 'What do I care about? What change am I seeking to make? What is mine to do? Where, when and how will I put my boldness into action?'

Your willingness to answer these questions creates the world of possibilities. The truth is, possibilities are everywhere you look, unless you're waiting for someone else to mend the broken world first. Whoever you think these heroes and heroines are, they are not coming. They trust *you* can do it. You can boldly lead in the world, in your world on the edge, and make a real difference.

Do you trust you can do it?

ONE
Paradox Of The World

O ur world is beautiful, inspiring and undeni-ably promising. It shows all the achievements of human genius and creativity. In our world, human innovation has redefined what it means to live, work, express oneself and connect with others.

Medical advancements have pushed the boundaries of our human life. Intelligent technological products and services are shaping our modern existence, opening possibilities for comfort and speed that inspire excitement and bold aspirations. The internet, a limitless digital space, bridges distances, creating a network of ideas, communities and dreams. Innovative applications make it possible for us to care for ourselves and support others in need effortlessly. Spirit and dedication have expanded the limits of what was considered phys-ically and mentally possible for a human being.

Our world glows with the promise of boundless potential, painting a picture of a future where any-thing we dare to imagine seems achievable. It is noth-ing short of miraculous. On the flip side, our world is dangerous, saddening and utterly uncertain. It's a stage for turmoil and chaos. It's a terrain where the dissonant sounds of fear and distress echo in every corner, with human suffering and conflict casting long shadows over our collective existence. It's a place in which we continuously witness injustice, inequality and devastation impacting the shape of societies and ecosystems as existential threats question the very foundation of our humanity.

Climate screams stand as a reminder of our deeply broken relationship with nature. In fact, we are at war with nature, even though we may not call it so. Wars and conflicts rage, driven by deeply seated hatreds and mentally disturbed geopolitical ambitions, leav-ing despair that is irreparable, in the best-case sce-nario, for decades. The gap between privileged and marginalised is unrestrainedly deepening in front of our eyes, challenging the core values of human-ness. The digital realm, for all its wonders, serves as a battleground for misinformation, humiliation of people from their earliest age, cyber threats and chal-lenges to our perceptions of truth and ultimately trust in humankind.

Our world resounds with the cries of the oppressed and grieving, as well as the music of depraved minds and their decisions that seek to steer it in the direction that stands a great chance of destroying civilisation. It is nothing more than devastatingly fragile.

Yes, you've got it. Our world is a paradox, and like every paradox, it cannot be neatly divided into good and bad, light and darkness. Every spark carries a trace of shadow, and vice versa.

Just consider, for instance, how intelligent products and services have managed to make our lives incredibly comfortable in almost surreal ways, yet they also influence new generations in manners that will define an entirely different set of values around human connection – values that we may not completely like to experience as our future reality. Our world is strong; our world is vulnerable in a dance of creation and destruction. It is always both.

Let's pause for a moment and reflect on what this paradox really means.

Darkness

Even though it feels as if we all know what it means, data can deepen our understanding and our shock. It is enough to check some of the available sources on world conflicts and forced displacement to access figures that uncover the darker shades of our global home. As I write this, we have stepped into the second half of 2024. It's been nearly eight decades since the curtains closed on World War II. In an ideal scenario, we could have hoped this would mark the end of all conflict, but it didn't. The reality we face is far different.

Conflict Data Explorer reveals that every year, without exception, at least 150 armed conflicts erupt.[8] The echoes of war are a constant hum in the background of our daily lives. Depending on what your corner of the world is, this might be closer or further away from you personally, but the truth is, this isn't a hypothetical scenario for anyone. This is the reality of the world we live in.

As leaders in any system, as humans in any corner of this world, we must be aware of these facts. More shocking is that in calmer years, the number of conflicts rarely went below 100, making our world a place where peace is merely a visitor, not a permanent resident. Even the reduced number stands for more conflicts than there are countries in Europe, North America and South America all together.

This image is scary enough without us recognising the human element behind it, because each conflict, each clash is a story of fear, loss and grief with the epilogue at its best being refugees, asylum seekers, internally displaced and stateless people. If you're already feeling overwhelmed by what I'm sharing, I beg you to stay with this reality here on paper for a little longer. The devastating statistics in the UNHCR Global Trends report about people who have been forcibly displaced show in total over 117.3 million had suffered this at the end of 2023.[9] In other words, more than the entire population of countries such as Ecuador or The Netherlands were forced to flee because of wars, persecution and unrest. It's like every single person in a bustling nation waking up to find they can no longer live in their own home.

Every. Single. Person.

That means more than one person in every sixty-nine on Earth has been forced to escape in search of a safe environment.[10] At the time of writing, the Ukrainian–Russian conflict has turned millions of lives upside down, but this story isn't unique. In the Democratic Republic of Congo, Ethiopia and Myanmar, over a million people in each of these countries were forced to abandon their homes, fleeing unimaginable dangers. The year 2023 brought a renewed sense of fear and apprehension. The re-ignition of conflict between Israel and Palestine in October of that year only added to the tide of human suffering, and by mid-2024 we were witnessing shameful scenarios with more-than-devastating figures and intolerable sufferings.

Having lived through war at the age of twelve, I carry an imprint in my bones – a deep inner knowing that war can never be a well-intentioned leadership response. Yet my bones also compassionately understand that it can be a human reaction, however devastating. That's why it's crucial that we never look away or silently accept it, but instead take action, no matter the scale.

If no war is taking place geographically close to you, you may pretend that it's not happening, but it still is. These figures are reality, and a conservative one at best. As time passes by, we all might forget that these horrors exist, but they do. It is the reality of our global home.

In addition to these conflicts, we are at war with nature. We have designed our relationships with nature in a way that already does and seemingly will continue to add to our human suffering. Disasters like floods and storms are continuously forcing millions of people from their homes to find new places to live, often with nothing but the clothes on their backs, if they're lucky. The 2024 Global Report on Internal Displacement (GRID) tells us that at the end of 2023, there were 7.7 million people living this way across the world as a result of disasters.[11]

If you haven't already, I urge you to watch *The Letter*,[12] a captivating documentary that tells the story of five individuals, each representing marginalised groups in our important global environmental discussions. We see their journey from the Amazon, India, Senegal and Hawai'i to the Vatican to meet with the Pope and engage in a crucial dialogue regarding *Laudato Si'*, a powerful encyclical addressing the climate change crisis and biodiversity loss.

You'll hear the story of Arouna Kandé, who fled climate hardships in Senegal; Cacique Dadá, a protector of the Maró Indigenous lands in the Amazon; Ridhima Pandey, an ardent youth climate advocate from India; and Greg Asner and Robin Martin, committed biologists exploring Hawai'i's coral reef ecosystems. Each of these five individuals, deeply impacted by the climate crisis, represents an unheard voice in global discussions on this planetary challenge. They also reveal a common pattern: those most affected often lack representation at the decision-making table.

All these stories and statistics – as well as other equally disturbing ones in different areas of humanity that I haven't mentioned, but you may hold at the forefront of your mind – are more than a number. They represent a disrupted life, a dream on hold, a journey of survival, all existing in a dangerous, saddening and utterly uncertain world.

Light

Our world isn't just dark; it has a bright side too. Imagine standing on the edge of a breakthrough that echoes the very pulse of our planet. Along the vast coastline of Australia, where the ocean meets the land, researchers at RMIT University have unlocked a secret of the sea – the ability to harness the relentless power of ocean waves and convert it into clean, sustainable energy.[13]

Hold that image in your mind for a moment: the wild, chaotic dance of ocean waves. Now imagine those same waves being transformed into a sustainable energy source vital for our existence on this planet. This scenario goes beyond just a story of inspiring innovation and certainly deserves in-depth technical conversation, but that's neither my intention nor my expertise.

The reason I'm sharing this story is because I wish to invite you to consider it as a narrative of harmony and hope. It's about human creativity meeting the natural world's power, leading to solutions that not only impress, but also promise a future where we live in sync with our planet. This isn't just about technological achievement; it's a chapter in our ongoing story of learning to be in balance with nature, to coexist sustainably with the environment that sustains us.

While we're joining the rhythm of the waves at one end of the globe, the Masaka Kids Africana have found a new rhythm of life in dance, following Albert Einstein's poignant words: 'We dance for laughter, we dance for tears, we dance for madness, we dance for fears, we dance for hopes, we dance for screams, we

are the dancers, we create the dreams.'[14] This statement surely captures the essence of this group of
resilient children dancing their way into the hearts of
millions from the scenery of Masaka, Uganda.

Founded by Suuna Hassan, Masaka Kids Africana is
more than a dance group; it's a movement, a sanctu-
ary for the soul of the children, many of whom are
orphans due to war, famine and disease. Hassan envisioned a haven where they could find security, care
and a platform to express themselves. Breathing life
into Masaka Kids Africana must have been his personal big, bold game, the one that invited him to compete not only with the harsh external conditions of the
environment, but with himself as well, with his doubts
and limitations, and to eventually win over both.

It looks as if he's done a great job in those inner and
outer battles, because the success of these children is
far-reaching. The global attention given to them has
translated into vital funding. There are funds coming
in from their performances; there are donations coming in from around the world, all to ensure that the
children's basic needs are met – food, shelter, cloth-
ing and, crucially, education, as well as the care that
extends beyond physical needs, including emotional
support, essential given their background and their
stories. They have become more than a group of children dancing. Masaka Kids Africana is a life-changing
initiative, a living, breathing proof of the fact that

futures can be rewritten, making this world a place that's truly inspiring.

There are other places of inspiring transformations, one tiny home at a time. In the heart of Fredericton, the capital city of New Brunswick, one of Canada's ten provinces, Marcel LeBrun, a visionary entrepreneur, turned his success into hope for the local homeless.[15] After selling his company for a large sum, he embarked on a mission to change lives. Being a visionary, LeBrun created '12 Neighbours' – a unique community of ninety-nine tiny homes, each a promise of a dignified new beginning for the homeless.

Imagine that: ninety-nine doors opening to ninety-nine worlds, where once there were none. Ninety-nine sparks of hope for those who have been hopeless, without a roof over their heads for far too long. More than being about building houses, LeBrun's initiative is about creating futures that happen when the power of compassion transforms into action. This is a story of how one spark can create a revolution of kindness thanks to the mission of a man who believes in instilling a new sense of responsibility and pride in those who have been marginalised. It's a story of one man's journey to make a difference and a community's journey to find home again in the world that is hereby proven to be undeniably promising.

Both

In March 2023, I had a remarkable opportunity to experience first-hand the world as a paradox. It was neither good nor bad; it was simply both.

My own journey took me to the pulsating heart of Bangalore, India; a city full of innovation and dreams. I had the honour of delivering a bold leadership development programme for a client renowned for pioneering advanced solutions in technology. As I walked through their state-of-the-art laboratories, I was immersed in a world of visionary minds and cutting-edge creations.

One of the most striking moments was meeting an engineer – let's call him Raj. Raj was deeply involved in explaining to me the development of a revolutionary chip designed to help stroke patients. What captivated me was not just the chip's potential to transform neurology, but the deep passion and love Raj demonstrated in detailing the meticulous engineering work that went into creating this tiny yet life-altering device. His eyes sparkled with the pride of an inventor who knows the value of his creation, not just in terms of technology, but in its potential to improve human lives.

As I walked through the corridors, always accompanied by staff to ensure my smooth access, I couldn't help but reflect on the range of products around me.

Although I saw little, most likely understood even less, I knew there was so much more there with the potential to drastically change our human lives.

I paused for a moment to imagine the dreams and visions of these creators. How bold were their inventions? Did fear ever clutch their hearts, and what miracles emerged when they dared to step past it, walking on the edge of innovation? What inspired them to embrace even greater boldness and awaken their inner power to shape the external future?

The ever-present paradox of Bangalore quickly brought me back from my own reflections. As you wander through its streets, you cannot avoid being struck by a vivid duality, a city of contrasts that seems to represent the very essence of our world. Outside the cutting-edge laboratories, life moves in its most primal and exuberant form. Streets echo with the hustle and bustle of a loud, raw daily existence; too many family members balance on motorbikes, navigating through the dangerous dance of traffic. You get scared to your bones at the mere sight of it, and then some loud vehicle horn wakes you up from the shock every few seconds.

Here, the reality of survival plays out in evident contrast to the futuristic environment of technological innovation within the lab walls. I found this polarity deeply profound. It was like walking on the edge between worlds – one the meticulously organised corridors of innovation, and the other, vibrant streets of everyday struggle and perseverance. Bangalore, in its unique way, reflects the paradox of our world where the miracles of human achievement coexist with the rawness of human challenges.

Our world is a collection of contradictions. It's a place where beauty and danger coexist, stirring a range of emotions, from hope to despair. While at different times in our lives, we can certainly feel the diverse intensity of hope and despair depending on where most of our attention goes, the world by its nature has continuously been on the edge.

As much as we may want to fix a world on the edge, the paradox of our global home is inherently unsolvable. This isn't an issue – instead of demanding solutions, it calls for a deeper recognition of its full complexity. It's precisely this understanding of the world's essence that becomes our starting point for identifying the changes we care most about. From there, we can activate our bold leadership to turn those changes into reality.

KEY IDEAS

- The world is a paradox: astonishing achievements alongside devastating challenges.
- Global conflicts and environmental crises hit the least represented hardest.

- Hope and innovation thrive – proving resilience is possible.
- Beauty and struggle coexist; this complexity is unsolvable, but offers opportunity.
- As a leader, embrace the paradox, ignite bold change and shape a better future.

Your mirror moment

Provoke your thoughts with these questions:

1. What opportunities do you find in a world full of contradictions?

2. How does the paradox of the world influence your view of leadership success and failure?

3. How does recognising both the light and dark sides of the world shape your sense of responsibility as a leader?

TWO
Our Broken Workplace

While the world is on the edge, where are you?

If you are an organisational leader, you're most likely at work, because the workplace is where you live a large part of your life. I'm convinced that you will find this statement confronting as well as true. If you wish to challenge it, I invite you to break down a typical day of yours, including all you want or need to squeeze into it. You'll most likely see that more than half of your waking existence is dedicated to either working or thinking about your work, whether you like to admit it or not.

Myriads of studies have researched how the amount of time we work varies depending on parameters such as our gender, age, education and family situation, but they all seem to be revealing one common trend: over the years, we're all spending more and more time working.[16] The world's relentless pace has become faster now, and with it, we're expected to be more productive than ever before. There are no signs of any attempt to slow down – not from us and therefore not from the world, or vice versa.

In addition, the boundaries of work have blurred. Coaching female leaders in global big tech, I often hear them complain that ever since Covid, they have been working *from* home and *for* home. Double the work plus time spent thinking about work. Work never really ends. All there is, is this accelerating trend of *more* and *faster* leaving us little room for the rest of our life. In such a workplace design, what is the rest of our life and when do we get to have it? Some of my clients say that we have imprisoned ourselves in our work and we're doing the time willingly.

I've noticed that many leaders I work with are exhausted and they all too often experience moments of despair. They question the sustainability of this relentless paradigm and worry about how long they can maintain the pace while staying mentally and physically healthy. The way they verbalise this challenge may differ – how do I achieve life-work balance; how do I stay motivated; how do I recharge; when do I get some breathing time; how do I become more resilient; what do I really want long-term, etc? However they phrase it, I want to believe that what is really at the heart of all their concerns is:

- How do I navigate this ever-evolving fast-paced workplace context without losing sight of what makes me feel alive and what my true work is?

- Amid a lot of doing, what am I leaving behind?

The everyday reality is often more simplistic than my secret desire: they are blindly dedicating themselves to completing tasks from a never-ending list. While that might initially make them feel on top of their game, it ultimately gets in the way of them envisioning and committing to the change they deeply care about, the change that makes sense, the one that their bold identity has every potential to make happen.

Where is our approach to this microworld – our work-place – fundamentally broken? Is the real problem the relentless pace and the excessive number of hours, or the underlying reason why we commit to them?

Are you feeling more than just secure?

Our work plays an undeniable role in fulfilling the basic existential needs that give us a sense of security. At the beginning of his book *21 Lessons for the 21st Century*,[17] Yuval Noah Harari – an Israeli historian, philosopher, best-selling author and leading voice in global discussions about technology, ethics and human progress – speaks about the challenges we are faced with due to technological advancements such as AI, big data algorithms and bioengineering. His message is clear: while these topics may seem abstract or distant to many, the possibility of job losses due to technological progress is a concern that touches everyone deeply. It's not just about the risk of losing a job; it's about what that loss represents – a threat to our existential security and consequently, a threat to our dignified belonging in the world.

This is how we predominantly perceive our work, but it is more than a mere provision of existential security. It's a crucial element in defining something as important as our sense of self.

Think of situations when we're invited to introduce ourselves. We often discuss our profession, proving how deeply our work is intertwined with our self-concept. When we meet someone new, one of the first questions we ask tends to be, 'What job do you do?' I agree that this sometimes happens for lack of a better question, but in reality, if we know how to listen, someone's job can offer clues into their values, interests and background. Our work often becomes a core part of how we define ourselves.

Defining ourselves by our jobs has been around for a while – common surnames often originate from historical professions.[18] In Germany and Switzerland, the most prevalent surname is Müller, and in Ukraine, it's Melnik; both translate to 'miller'. Slovakia's most common last name is Varga, meaning 'cobbler'. In English-speaking countries like the UK, Australia, New Zealand, Canada and the US, Smith is the most common family name, referring to various professions such as blacksmiths or locksmiths. Dating back to ancient history, occupations were so pivotal to people's identities that they frequently became their actual names, which shows that work has had a profound impact on shaping personal and social identities through the ages.

The late Pope John Paul II in his encyclical *Laborem Exercens* grounded work in the very essence of human existence, claiming that it is one of the defining characteristics that differentiates humans from other living beings, whose activities for sustaining life cannot truly be called work.[19] He underlined that humans alone are capable of work, with work occupying a central role in our existence on Earth, saying, 'Thus, work bears a particular mark of man and of humanity, the mark of a person operating within a community of persons. And this mark decides its interior characteristics; in a sense it constitutes its very nature.'

Humans have the unique ability to engage in work that is not just for survival, but also for fulfilling a deeper purpose. It's not merely an activity; it is an expression of our nature, of who we are and why we are here.

We have the choice to realise the deepest aspirations of our soul through our work, making it a source of our sense of aliveness. Sometimes that choice comes with the risk of making a radical career change, even when it looks like we've got everything one could ask for.

In her book *Working Identity*, Herminia Ibarra, an expert in career development and leadership, tells a story of a client under the pseudonym Pierre Gerard.[20] Pierre was a thirty-eight-year-old best-selling French author and successful psychotherapist who felt a growing sense of dissatisfaction and lack of fulfilment in his work, leading him to seriously embrace his interest in spirituality. Eventually, he decided to leave his medical career and fully embrace life as a monk.

Not every path has to be this radical, but I will argue that to find aliveness in what you do, you must lose security. Terence McKenna – an American visionary, ethnobotanist, mystic, philosopher and author, as well as a pioneering voice in discussions about the expansion of human consciousness – expresses it much more powerfully when speaking about nature loving our courage as we dream the impossible dream and rewarding us by removing obstacles from our way: 'This is how magic is done. By hurling yourself into the abyss and discovering it's a feather bed.'[21]

We often think that hurling oneself into the abyss is only for the seemingly crazy, irrational or bold individuals who leave corporate jobs to start their own businesses, as though there is no trade-off between feeling alive and playing it safe once they exit the system. This is far from the truth. First, we are always part of some system. Second, the systems we create ourselves hold more tension between security and aliveness than those who haven't dared to do so might imagine. Third, as humans, we can't escape the tension between existential security and what ignites deep passion in our lives. In fact, we mustn't, as navigating this tension could be considered the essence of human growth.

Do you choose passion?

What are you deeply passionate about in your work? If you cannot immediately respond, it's high time you found either a coach to help you explore the answer or the courage to leave your job.

That said, before you become demoralised, know that you are not an exception if you are walking the corridors of your organisation feeling passionless. In fact, you might be nice and normal in the world as we know it today. According to some common beliefs about passion, 'Nice, normal people don't have it'. This is one of the key points Larry Smith, a professor of economics at the University of Waterloo in Canada, made in his 2011 TEDx talk 'Why you will fail to have a great career'.[22] Another reason for betraying our own passion on the list is: 'I would do this, but I'm not weird'. That leads many people to stay safely away from their passions to the point where, sadly, they never find out what makes them weird.

Weird or normal, without passion, your potential will remain dormant. In my keynotes I often quote Larry Smith's statement: 'Passion is the thing that will help you create the highest expression of your talent',[23] after which I ask the audience: 'What is it about your industry and your job that really makes your heart sing?' A few might have an immediate answer, but most do not. Instead, they pause to reflect, likely carrying this question with them long after the keynote is over.

This is because we continually convince ourselves that choosing a sense of safety and security over passion is a reasonable decision, until we slowly buy into the perspective that it is the only choice we've got. Sounds familiar? Despite us frequently hearing advice to follow our dreams and passions, a part of us views this path as too irrational, too unreasonable, too bold and too risky for our current situation, so we shy away from even exploring what truly brings joy to our hearts.

Some people are unafraid of being weird. These are the 'passionpreneurs' – people who blend their passions with entrepreneurship transforming it into a thriving business. For me, being a passionpreneur is really a mindset more than anything else. It's a choice to put into action the courage, confidence and creativity to pursue what makes you feel most alive. This choice must come from your conviction that work is supposed to be a means to realise the deepest love of your soul.

Two adventurous spirits come to my mind when I think of this conviction. Imagine aiming to visit nothing less than every country in the world, many of them being places where the average person might hesitate to set foot. Kristijan Ilicic's Travel Experiences,[24] covering over 190 countries at the time of writing, reflect a commitment to stepping outside his comfort zone to visit some of the world's most dangerous places, embracing diverse cultures with respect and curiosity. Coming from the small European country of Croatia, Kristijan has journeyed across both Americas, large parts of Africa and Asia, the Far East, and even places like Afghanistan, Somalia, Yemen and some of the most secluded countries in the world like Turkmenistan.

He has transformed his love for travel into a thriving career. One aspect of this is the travel agency he founded, offering unique experiences grounded in his extensive expertise, but his true mission, I believe, lies in sharing his stories from across the globe. Through his content, he challenges prejudices and biases about different nationalities and their homelands, presenting the truth as he sees it. His goal is to reshape the narrative around countless global locations and cultures, one story at a time.

Speaking of travels, ever heard of *The Atlas of Beauty*?[25] A photographer from Romania, Mihaela Noroc, has spent over a decade photographing women in more than 100 different countries and collecting their inspiring stories in her book. She says she is dreaming of it being a lifelong project that promotes the beautiful side of humanity and makes a contribution, no matter how small, to a better world.

Mihaela takes photos of women in the true authenticity of their physical and life conditions, focusing on their eyes, which tell their story of courage and commitment. As a mother of a young daughter, she has made it her mission to show female diversity in all its power and beauty, underlining that beauty has no bounds, and that the diversity of this world is here to be cherished rather than taken as an argument for conflicts.

At the time of writing this book, Mihaela Noroc has announced her stunning follow-up collection, *The Power of Women*,[26] including 500 portraits from over sixty countries such as Japan, India, Peru, Namibia and the United States. Critics have praised the book as yet another powerful celebration of the courage, resilience and unparalleled depth of women's beauty.

Notice the conviction that both these people bring to their work. From these two brief descriptions, you can realise what they stand for and how they apply their core commitment to what they do. They are not part of any organisation (even though they may work with many), and as such, they are not leaders shaping the world by their position, but they are leaders by conviction, inspiring with their passion for the change that they create.

Way too many of our workplace experiences do not mirror the passionpreneurial mindset, which has nothing to do with exciting travels. I'm sure that a lot of the places Kristijan and Mihaela travel to, many of us would instantly consider the least exciting to visit. The passionpreneurial mindset has everything to do with understanding our potential on a deeper level and having the courage to allow it to manifest – being bold enough to choose our passion in the work that we do.

Do you have a passionpreneurial mindset?

Back to a different reality – what's happening with passion for most working people today? Judging by Gallup's *State of the Global Workplace Report* 2024, 'The voice of the world's employees',[27] passion certainly has disappeared with 77% of the global workforce either non-engaged or actively disengaged. That sounds like a huge number of passionless people in their workplaces, or even worse, not only passionless, but also stressed, angry, worried, sad and lonely.

There are many other worrying pieces of data from surveys on stress at work affecting mental wellbeing. You can read that information and see dry and boring statistics, or you can listen to what such figures communicate. They speak of silenced joy, the eroded sense of true belonging and personal lives that bear the weight of an invisible yet oppressive burden. They remind us of the number of people in the workplace, our microworld – perhaps someone we know, maybe even ourselves – yearning for aliveness.

These internal battles within our workplaces – where we spend most of our waking hours – are, in their own way, a reflection of another troubling image of our world. The real questions for me are:

- How did we come to the point where we have to discuss our workplaces from the perspective of mental health issues that deplete our very essence, rather than from the perspective of our passionate existence?

- If being a passionpreneur represents one extreme, doesn't the situation in which we experience mental health issues because of work appear to be its exact opposite?

- Why do we tend to normalise this scenario much more than the other?

Before you continue reading, I want you to pause and reflect. Have you started normalising this scenario? Do you feel that mental health issues arising from work are no longer an urgent concern, while the idea of turning passion into a career seems almost like a fantasy? I'm not asking this to pass judgement, nor for you to judge yourself. I'm asking because it's crucial to understand how your mindset towards the workplace might be stopping you from recognising the bold changes you truly want to make. What are you normalising and what are you completely excluding when it comes to the context of our workplace as a microworld that affects us all?

In his whitepaper *The Spirit of Leadership*,[28] Robert (Bob) J Anderson, chief knowledge officer at Leadership Circle®, best explains where our approach to our workplace is fundamentally damaged:

'The pursuit of safety and economic success, while necessary to support the journey, often become ends unto themselves [sic]. The reality that we are spiritual beings on an evolutionary journey has been effectively and completely excluded from the world of work to the detriment of the individual, the workplace, and the world.'

Trading our passions for our sense of safety and security is like letting fear triumph over love – a choice that always bears consequences, despite the convincing arguments from our minds. As Bob Anderson says, safety is necessary to support the journey, but when we make safety *the* journey, which seems to have become our standard approach, we get disconnected from the path and anyone we meet along it, including ourselves.

One of the consequences of being disconnected from our passions and ourselves is that we can easily become disconnected from each other. Helen Keller, an American author and political activist, once said, 'Alone we can do so little; together we can do so much.'[29] Making a bigger impact collectively must have been our inspiration for creating teams in the first place.

The 2024 calendar on my work desk, created by Designed Learning,[30] a company founded by Peter Block, an American author and speaker renowned in the field of community building, emphasises that relationships are the delivery system for achieving anything significant. Similarly, the Organisation and Relationship Systems Coaching (ORSC) approach to team coaching sees relationships as the currency that runs organisations.[31] What these perspectives share is the emphasis on connection and collaboration in service of more meaningful work and greater impact. When a sense of security is prioritised over our passion for our work, we risk becoming disconnected from our souls, our service and each other.

Playing it safe, we drift away from passion, yet we easily ride the wave of drive. Drive is supported so strongly within organisations that some of them have it listed among their values. It's something that will never cease to surprise me. At its best, drive is an immature version of passion. Instead of unlocking potential for the greater good, drive awakens competition where there shouldn't be any, exhausts us in the long run and reinforces disconnection.

Disconnected from each other, we stand a high chance of becoming what Margaret Heffernan, a writer, keynote speaker and professor of practice at the University of Bath School of Management in the UK, calls 'super-chickens' in one of her brilliant TED Talks.[32] She speaks about William Muir, a Purdue University biologist who conducted an experiment segregating chickens based on their egg production and grouping average egg-laying chickens together.

He also grouped together a prolific egg-laying flock of 'super-chickens'. Keeping these chickens in their groups for two generations, Muir found that the average chickens consistently produced eggs, while in the super-chickens' group, only three survived. The rest of the group had pecked each other to death.

I'm sure you've come across super-chickens in your workplace – people keeping their colleagues down so that they can stay on top. Perhaps you're one of them. In the environment where security rules over passion, it's not all that difficult to adopt competition over collaboration. We somehow end up behaving as if Keller had said: 'To stay safe and secure, alone I must do better than you.'

Passion inspires a different perspective. With a passionate leader, we see a future full of possibilities that we want to be part of. Passion creates the territory for connection and collaboration because it allows us to see and hear those who embody it at their deepest level. We see their passion, we believe in the change they care about and we want to get on board. True passion is mobilising.

I remember working with a group of seasoned leaders in one of the European Union (EU) institutions. To be completely honest, I had my own views on public servants' work, both on the national and EU levels, considering them simply as bureaucrats. However, working with these individuals radically shifted my mindset.

We had a one-and-a-half-day programme exploring personal stories, core values, coaching skills, and developing and communicating leadership visions. Imagine a team of public servants standing at the front of the room one by one, declaring their personal leadership vision, communicating what they believe in, what they stand for and the culture they wish to inspire as leaders. It was a conversation that they had never had before. It was an opportunity to reintroduce themselves to the others.

One of the participants was a firm believer in EU integration. She said, 'You can list reasons why we exist, but what we're truly here for is a peacekeeping mission through our mere existence. The more integrated we are, the more successful we'll be in this for many years to come.' These are probably the only words I remember from her speech, but they are enough for me to vividly recall the passion with which she spoke and the conviction she displayed while advocating for the future she believed in. I remember the other participants' reaction to her – colleagues who had known her for years were seeing the spark in her eyes as if for the first time. Quickly, they understood – it had always been there, but now they too were able to see it.

From the margins of the room, I observed the participants, feeling a palpable connection and mobilisation around her vision. Isn't that the purpose of leadership, to mobilise others around your vision so they can see their own within it? These people weren't competing;

they were united, ready to care about what she cared about. They were connected to her, to themselves and to each other. They even got me connected to the idea of EU public service, shifting my long-held superficial perception.

Do you have a coaching consciousness?

Witnessing such examples makes it even more heart-breaking to read the previously mentioned 2024 Gallup *State of the Global Workplace Report*, which highlights the high levels of non-engagement and active disengagement among employees, clearly showing that those who are not engaged are less likely to feel a connection to their organisation.[33] We need to act on this reality by changing the conversation and finding a deeper way of connecting to everyone, including ourselves.

Gallup proposes a solution: train managers to become effective coaches.[34] I couldn't agree more. In a world flooded by technological advancement where work never really stops, learning the coaching language may be our last line of defence against disconnecting and losing touch with our humanity. That's because the language of coaching fundamentally shapes how we show up, for both ourselves and others.

As a coach, I know that the true power of coaching lies in connection – connecting deeply with the person in front of us. We see them, regardless of what they bring to the table. We hear them, which helps them become deeply curious and passionate about their own identity, work and legacy, because curiosity begets curiosity. Passion begets passion. Through learning coaching skills, we actually develop a different way of being: a mindset of boldness, connection and curiosity. It's what I call our coaching consciousness.

Coaching consciousness helps us cure the disconnection disease that has become so prevalent in the workplace – provided we are bold enough to be and act in a new way:

- Being genuinely curious about what we and our communities deeply care about.

- Being uncompromisingly connected with ourselves and others on a deep human level.

- Putting our boldness into action to continuously challenge the 'normal' that contradicts our connection to the deepest commitment of our soul and to one another and hinders our curiosity.

Here is the thing – or should I say the risk? Coaching consciousness will ask us to stop being resistant to vulnerability. The road from disconnection to connection requires the risk of exposure.

During one of my sessions with the top leadership team of a global organisation, I invited the participants to stay in our two-day conversation with an open heart. One of them responded, 'We don't do open heart. This is not how we normally speak to each other around here.' That told me a lot about their usual approach of playing it safe in interactions. We needed to take a step back and introduce a foundational principle that I once heard from a wonderful coach and colleague: 'Open your heart before you open your mouth.'[35]

Before you consider it harsh, please notice that what this simple yet powerful invitation really does is to encourage the development of social awareness and empathy as part of our emotional intelligence. By stepping into other people's shoes before judging them, we build a genuine sense of connection. Without this sense of connection, the need for safety deepens, bringing drive to the forefront, increasing isolation and diminishing our chances of giving ourselves permission to create what we so passionately care about. It's hard to create anything while preoccupied with our lost sense of either safety or security or both; all we're then trying to do is to regain them.

To refer back to the story, those leaders did indeed open their hearts. They engaged in conversations with genuine curiosity, courage and utmost compassion for one another. This shift required me, as their facilitator, to model vulnerability first – exposing my own raw and real self for the sake of their learning. This created a safe space for them to follow suit.

Part of us always remains childlike; no matter what we are told, we are far more likely to follow the actions we see modelled. Ultimately, we follow leaders for what they do, not for what they say they will do, so we need them to take action first.

My team and I have trained many leaders in developing coaching consciousness as part of cultivating a bold leadership culture within their organisations. We have seen how coaching consciousness offers a promising route away from isolation – both from ourselves and others – and towards the excitement of what we can achieve together when connected. Being together yet disconnected, we can hardly ever mobilise others around the change we so passionately seek to create.

What makes you adapt-eager?

I have spoken a lot about passion here, yet as you've likely noticed, in the workplace, the focus often isn't on passion. We don't discuss how to be more passionate; instead, we talk about how to be more – as I love to call it – adapt-able.

Today's workplace demands that we quickly mobilise our capacity to adapt to emerging changes. There are so many; they come so fast and so often. It's therefore no wonder that 'adapt-ability' is frequently mentioned as the single most important skill for leaders.

Within organisational settings, being adapt-able could be defined as responding swiftly to market shifts, new technologies and consumer trends – essentially, to a multitude of organisational signals for change, both internal and external. Adapt-ability is crucial for maintaining a competitive edge and ensuring personal and organisational success. You've likely heard all this repeatedly in your organisation, perhaps even to the point of irritation.

Here's what I've noticed whenever I'm invited to discuss change by my clients. When I offer my keynote, 'The game of change: How to be a bold player', the sponsors tend to express a desire for a single outcome – they want their audience to leave the event being more adapt-able to upcoming changes.[36] However, by the end of our conversation, more often than not, we come closer to this perspective: their audience is already perfectly able to adapt, but they might not be willing, let alone eager to do so.

Here's how I see the distinction: as humans, we're naturally capable of adapting, though the pace varies and practice helps improve this skill. Facing challenges gradually strengthens our ability to change. However, beyond just adapting, there's a conscious choice to embrace change when needed, which I call 'adapt-willingness' – a mindset of ongoing openness to new experiences and influences.

While we're all capable of change, not everyone is willing to embrace it. I love how Pippi Longstocking, a character created by Swedish author Astrid Lindgren, speaks of courage and confidence in facing the new: 'I have never tried that before, so I think I should definitely be able to do that.'[37] I'm one of those people that always connects with Pippi's mindset, because I believe nothing stays the same. However, while it's hard to argue against constant change, it's perfectly normal to want things to remain a bit more stable. The relentless pace of change in the workplace today can often lead to what feels like adaptation fatigue.

How do we distinguish between not being willing to change and simply being tired of it? The key is whether the change resonates with us. If our primary motivation for being at work is security and not passion, very few changes will feel meaningful. Resistance to change often stems from a lack of motivation, which is rooted in why we're in the workplace in the first place. That's why in cultivating adapt-willingness – our openness to change on both an individual and collective level – we need to revisit the question 'Why are we here?'

I want to take this concept of adapt-willingness even further, additionally empowering our attitude to change. Our welcoming change isn't just about responding to it; it's about creating it. It's a proactive mindset in which we're always looking for ways to improve things. This means seeing possibilities everywhere, opportunities to create something better than what already exists.

Here, adapt-willingness evolves into what I call 'adapt-eagerness' – the passion to change things, even what's considered normal because it's always been that way, despite making little sense. Adapt-eagerness means embracing change enthusiastically before it becomes necessary.

However, even when we're the ones initiating change, we need to be clear on one thing: we still have to continuously adapt, which can feel like stepping away from the familiar and letting go of our sense of security. I also don't want to suggest that we should blindly welcome every change. Recently, I listened to an interview with Neha Sangwan, an internal medicine physician, author and corporate communication expert, and something she said really resonated: 'There's a pace at which we are now moving that is not in sync with our own biology. A person will reach a point where it's too much as uniquely as their own fingerprint.'[38]

I've been reflecting on the global pace of change in the workplace and within our personal leadership journeys. One thing I'm sure of: once we master the limiting inner beliefs about our worthiness – which we'll explore later in this book – we can better understand the right pace for ourselves. This is a pace that Neha suggests supports our most authentic and bold selves. While I'm unsure how to slow down the world's pace – or if we should – I do know we have a responsibility to pause when we feel out of sync to allow ourselves time to recover before moving forward. We have the ability through honest self-reflection to discern whether we're truly out of sync or just afraid.

It's not about adapting to given change at any cost, especially when it either feels more harmful than helpful or doesn't feel meaningful. Sometimes, it's about resisting the current pace to create the change we truly need. Questioning change can be in itself the first step towards creating it.

Whether you are asked to embrace changes or are initiating the changes you want to see and be, it requires a high level of eagerness to adapt over and over again. Regardless of your view on the pace of the external world, the need for adapt-eagerness is undeniable. It will significantly influence your leadership and directly impact the success of the changes you seek to create and the difference you hope to make.

But let's take a moment to step back – do you truly know what change you seek to create?

KEY IDEAS

- Work dominates our lives, with increasingly blurred boundaries between the personal and professional.

- While work provides security, balancing it with passion is key to aligning it with a deeper life purpose.

- Prioritising drive over passion in our workplaces breeds disengagement and disconnection.

- In a highly volatile environment, go beyond adapting to change by embracing adapt-eagerness – a proactive, passionate approach to leading meaningful change.

- Cultivate coaching consciousness – curiosity, connection and boldness – to heal workplace disconnection and inspire transformative leadership.

Your mirror moment

Provoke your thoughts with these questions:

1. How has the relentless pace of your work affected your sense of meaning and purpose?

2. In the midst of your busy work environment, how do you stay connected to what makes you feel alive and focused on your true values?

3. With all the tasks you're doing, what are you really leaving behind? How might redefining productivity affect your legacy?

4. How much are you giving up passion for the security of your job? Do you think one always has to come at the expense of the other? How is that affecting you?

5. What would it mean to bring passion back into your work? What kind of leader could you become if you embraced what truly excites and inspires you?

Then use these to start bold conversations in your workplace:

1. Is our drive pushing the team towards real achievement, or is it quietly undermining our ability to collaborate and create? How does this affect us in the long run?

2. How could embracing coaching principles like curiosity, connection and boldness change how we approach our work? Are we ready to incorporate more of these? What would that look like, and how would it benefit both us and the organisation?

3. Are we just adapting to changes or are we eager to create them? What impact could we have if we actively looked for opportunities to innovate instead of waiting for change to become necessary? How can we shift from being leaders who react to change to becoming leaders who create change?

THREE
Your Landscape
For Change

The landscape in which you lead is where you begin to discover the difference you're eager to make. Starting with the wider context of the world, then narrowing the lens to the workplace and zooming in even further to your specific context, you uncover the landscape where you have the opportunity to create the change you wish to see. This is your most immediate reality – one shaped by global events, workplace trends and your personal life. Your leadership landscape is your starting point – your circle of impact.

As you examine your leadership landscape, what might you see? Reflecting trends in the workplace, some issues might be on your agenda: the need to be faster, more cost-efficient, more productive, more digital, more AI-driven, more diverse and inclusive, more creative, more sustainable, or perhaps all of the above. Amidst these demands, it's easy to lose sight of the changes that truly matter to you. You may find yourself navigating yet another restructuring, innovation initiative, culture shift or some other imposed change project, all while motivating others – and sometimes yourself – to adapt rather than resist.

What else might you feel? The emotional intensity of the global times in which you live and lead, alongside the intensity of personal moments and experiences that uniquely shape your leadership landscape. Let's explore how all of this comes together and what opportunities it presents.

The pressure of relentless change

As you navigate your leadership landscape, the demands for constant improvement and adaptation can feel intense. The pressure of relentless change can be a harsh reality to embrace, which brings to my mind an interesting conversation I had with a client in the banking industry.

'You need to come in and talk to them about change,' he said as we agreed on my keynote for the organisation's top 150 leaders.

'What are you hoping for me to tell them?' I asked.

'Tell them that change is constant. They need to stop waiting for it to go away because it won't. That's not how this world and the organisations in it operate anymore. We are and will remain in ongoing transformation.'

'Shall I invite them to fall in love with change?' I asked enthusiastically. I then noted the client's facial expression, which suggested that, amidst all that embracing of change, the idea of actually loving change sounded too ambitious.

He is not my only client holding on to this paradox. You are likely feeling the same in your personal leadership landscape, but if our world is one of ongoing transformation, falling in love with change is exactly how ambitious we need to be. After all, my client is right – change won't go away.

Our individual landscapes, regardless of the wide range of specifics, have one commonality: they resemble permanent white water through which we have to paddle, ready to get bounced out and equally ready to bounce back. While you may already have a sense of how this feels based on the metaphor, here's a little bit more about what this concept of permanent white water actually means.

In his book *Learning as a Way of Being*, Peter B Vaill explores the constant state of uncertainty and turbulence of our times.[39] The only thing that seems to be certain is the one many of us are not super fond of and that is the likelihood change will continue to accelerate due to increasing complexity and interdependence in the world. This is what Vaill calls 'permanent white water'. Although we can't predict the exact course of these changes or identify hidden obstacles, we must know how to operate at the level of seasoned rafters, anticipating being thrown into the white water and recovering instead of succumbing to shock and drowning.

Retreating into resistance is always an alternative, as long as you know that while it may be a natural response to the high-pressure environment, resistance won't turn white water into a peaceful lake. Resistance won't block any change long-term, but it may well block your ability to notice your chance to make a valuable difference in it.

Nonetheless, I've seen some leaders persist in choosing this alternative. We could say that it blinds them to the fact that whatever the landscape in which they lead looks like, it inevitably holds transformation imperative. In PwC's 26th Global CEO survey, nearly 40% of CEOs thought their company would fail economically a decade from now if it resisted change and continued on its current path.[40]

The change in the world is accelerating. Leaders, therefore, need to build an ongoing transformation capability that enables their organisations to challenge themselves and keep evolving and adapting as conditions change. To do so, they need to build the transformation capability to challenge and evolve themselves first.

These are powerful facts, but what's the reality? Away from renowned surveys and looking instead into some simple coaching conversations with leaders, we can quickly pick up the common sentiment of most of them: they are fed up with adapting to changes that they never asked for. All they want is for them to stop, together with their accompanying discomfort.

In addition to the workplace trends, our global home has its reflection in our most immediate reality – the landscape in which we lead. Current disruptions are not only of a technological nature. Whether the world's turbulent events are being addressed or not, their emotional impact is largely felt.

Look at the impact of war and other conflicts. They're not just disrupting labour markets but human lives, and they're affecting our individual and collective emotional space. Think of global teams and how such disruptions shape the collective psyche, influencing everything from employee morale to the strategic priorities of organisations. Think of your family, your friends, perhaps even yourself if you've built homes and lives in places where peace no longer reigns at the moment. Geopolitical tensions, economic instability and social distress reach into the heart of our personal and professional lives, leaving no one intact.

Emotionally, these are deeply painful times in which we live and lead. This may be a universal truth for every generation, but that doesn't lessen the intensity of what we feel, and it doesn't stop there. Beyond the global crises and the disruptive demands of the workplace, the landscape in which we lead is also shaped by the nuances of our intimate personal reality – parts of our life that perhaps few people know about. It holds stories of our own world on the edge. I shared one of mine in the introduction to this book. Now let me tell you about a related but more recent episode.

My world on the edge

It was the beginning of July 2024, a sunny Friday morning far too bright to dedicate to a meeting with the person who had prematurely darkened my horizon one Tuesday nearly thirteen years prior. That was exactly how long we had not seen each other.

Over a decade had passed, time in which we both must have constructed additional stories about each other beyond those formed during our long-gone professional relationship.

He was the chairman I reported to in an oil and gas company. In December 2011, my corporate career ended abruptly when he ordered the security manager to physically remove me from the office. If you have read the prologue of my book *Bold Reinvented*, you'll have found the story described as an episode from my School of Hard Knocks where I explore a pivotal shift in my career that launched me on a profound journey of personal and leadership growth, ultimately reshaping my work and defining what I now embrace as my personal and professional reality. I believe in endless possibilities, but that day, it was as though every possibility had slammed shut. I felt my dignity was stripped away and my expelled body sensed the closure of all paths.

Fast forward nearly thirteen years and we met again. Thanks to the attorney on the other side who skilfully navigated a justice system overly flexible with its principles, he had successfully avoided court appearances for years. Finally, there we were, standing in the long, dark, hot corridor of the Municipal Labour Court in Zagreb, in a building called The Palace of Justice.

Just a week prior, I had returned from Barcelona feeling centred in my body; you could say I was as somatically transformed as possible after attending a four-day course at The Strozzi Institute. The leadership development curriculum I had treated myself to had worked its magic, and I felt my body differently positioned in all three major dimensions that the course taught me about: length, width and depth.

In essence, my posture now conveyed personal dignity, my stance was wide enough to assert my space and establish my boundaries, and my centre was aligned with my commitment in life that had just got a new wording: I *am* a commitment to risk-taking for a world of bold leadership and human dignity. Thanks to this rewiring, there was one essential way in which my demeanour was entirely different from before: it no longer gave away its power in front of this person – a change I felt acutely the moment our eyes met.

'Good morning,' I greeted him as he walked down the corridor.

'Good morning,' he responded with a broad grin, approaching me with his hand outstretched. 'I hear you've got a successful business.'

Had my mind been in the lead, it might have replied with a bitter remark such as, 'What an entry after thirteen years when you seem to have successfully eradicated me together with my work!', but that wasn't the answer my current identity genuinely preferred. Standing there, powered by newfound somatic wisdom, I simply smiled and replied, 'Yes, I've built a very fulfilling business.' He then became curious about the markets in which I work and talked to me as if we had been enjoying a good cuppa last time we met and were continuing the pleasant chat. It went on until the judge stopped this play by calling us into the courtroom.

As we entered, I felt my husband's gentle touch on my hand, offering a quiet affirmation of my newly discovered centredness with a silent message: 'You've got this.' He, who has been both my loyal attorney and loving partner in this risk-taking journey, surely understood the discomfort of the challenge ahead, right there in that little courtroom with its stale air and old battles. There I was, safeguarding my integrity. There he was – my former chairman – fighting for his reputation. We certainly did not share the same values, ones which hold that your integrity is your biggest reputation, and if you have to fight for it, it's a battle you've already lost. As humans, we can and will make a mess, but we can always choose to clean it up.

As my husband and I took our seats, a flood of memories washed over me – countless courtrooms we had sat in, the myriad of rulings we had received. Some brought joy, pride and a sense of justice, while others left us with tears, anger, disappointment and despair.

The world has consistently and unsuccessfully tried to remind me of my powerlessness in front of a big organisation. 'There's nothing you can do about it!' I've heard it shout this belief – one my entire being has been refusing to embrace as a truth for years. Each experience has underscored the silent pact my husband and I made not to yield in the face of a daunting system, but to persistently stand our ground, come what may.

There have been moments when respecting this pact was really hard. Being eight months pregnant with my son and walking into courtrooms where, as part of the defence strategy, I was offended, even mocked for the rights I was demanding was a harrowing experience. Listening to lies being told by some of the people who had been close to me and whom I'd deeply trusted, watching that trust turn to dust at moments when I most needed to rely on them, was devastating. I saw others unable to passionately tell the complete truth for fear of losing their jobs. Understanding this did not decrease my pain.

I have experienced the power of a big system asserting its right to follow court rulings when and how it wanted to. At a certain stage in the process, we lost one case and I was obligated to settle huge amounts of costs for the organisation's lawyer. I did not have the full amount, so as per my former organisation's request, the court blocked my monthly salaries to take the payback. In addition to that, they sent an official to our house to write down the property they could take away in exchange, just a few days before Christmas of 2020. I could not help but think how this was reminiscent of being kicked out of the organisation just before Christmas in 2011.

I also remember being in a winning position and watching the opposing party simply disregard the decisions they disliked. My only option was to initiate yet another court case in a country system that offers little in terms of trust, safety or civil protection.

These and many other situations have caused tremendous continuous emotional discomfort, as well as significant anxiety about the still ongoing uncertainty of the future. I have been deeply worried and afraid. There are some very real reasons for feeling that way: a financial risk of covering legal costs if we lose after so many years; a risk to relationships within our family – questioning whether our bond is strong enough to endure the challenges of this edge; and even a risk to physical safety – wondering if someone will be provoked to cross the line, which I'm aware can happen in a power-dominated context. All of this has been and still is a harsh reality for me in a world that relentlessly reminds me of my seeming insignificance against the power of the system: you would love to see it changed, but there's nothing you can do about it.

The discomfort existed elsewhere, too. My former chairman's curiosity went in the right direction – I did develop my practice in a global market, but this was partly because many local doors were closed to me and my professional services. In my first years of navigating this challenging path, the rejection only deepened the shame I carried. I had the choice to drown in that shame, witnessing doors being slammed more or less politely in my face, or to look beyond the closed doors and discover many others that were open.

At one point, I was warned that my persistence in walking on this edge would not look good for my business and might damage my image. However, given that you're now reading the expanded version of this story in my second book, you can guess that I chose to embrace the risk boldly. This choice might seem odd to those with a different worldview, but in my mental framework, as much as standing up for my integrity presents substantial risks, damaging my reputation is not one of them.

Nonetheless, discomfort, an inexorable absence of the sense of both safety and security, has been my faithful companion. At moments, it has felt just like

Jeff Foster – a British spiritual teacher and author – describes it in his interview on the *Life Without a Centre* podcast called 'Insights at the edge': 'Everything feels out of sync, out of your hands, out of balance and out of control.'[41] I've experienced this many more times than I would have wanted, something akin to a painful sense of regret in both my belly and my chest, as well as confusion about what's next because both my present and my past have disintegrated.

Sometimes when things feel this way, the wisest decision is to continue trusting as you take your next steps, one foot after the other. That's precisely what I've been doing for the past thirteen years – walking along this precarious edge. Along the way, I've learned how to be with it: on some days like a prisoner with heavy shackles on, some like a queen with her precious crown and on others blissfully unaware of its presence.

The game-changing moment came when I stopped seeking emotional relief and began to harness this discomfort, channelling it into a creative force for the change I deeply care about. You could say that I've turned the disturbing aspect of the edge I was walking on into my ally. The ORSC approach to coaching teams in organisations and other systems teaches this as one of the key metaskills or ways of being: 'disturbance as my ally, an invaluable teacher in all the circumstances ensuring my growth'.[42]

Choosing growth empowered me, and empowerment is my most effective response to anyone trying to exert power over me. Embracing this mindset not only creates peace and a sense of security within me, but also sharpens my focus on impactful work in an otherwise deeply unsettling landscape. In other words, it's making sure that my world on the edge ultimately makes sense to me.

Drawing inspiration from my walk on the edge, I focus on creating work that is deeply fulfilling for me. While some might see this as building a successful business, it's much more profound than that. It's about understanding the change that I deeply care about, then finding my way to lead that change in the outside world, allowing my actions to shape my identity along the path.

Some comment on how skilfully I've built my brand over the years. While I don't mind it being called a brand, it's essential to understand what it truly represents – my commitment to creating change I wish to see in the world. More precisely in organisations that I believe have tremendous power to shape the world and our experience of life. Brand or business, what I'm essentially doing is claiming my arena where I bring my bold agency as I walk along the edge that often seems to suggest I have none.

Claiming your arena

It's overly simplistic to believe that a single narrative can define the edge of your world. While it can dramatically influence it, life's complexity far exceeds such a narrow view. One story might dominate at times, but there are undoubtedly other important narratives in your personal leadership environment – your landscape for change.

Rather than reducing your world on the edge to one key story, I'm inviting you to read between the lines of many of your stories and notice a consistent theme – they're all likely to speak about what matters most to you. Pause for a moment. Breathe deeply. Picture the entire landscape in which you lead. It's your starting point, your circle of impact. Standing at this starting point, ask yourself, where to from here? The answer is right into your arena, your specific circle of influence, once you identify what and where that is.

What is your arena? Where do you bring your bold agency?

Your arena is the specific space in your leadership landscape in which you decide to put your bold leadership into action. It's a space in which activating your agency makes complete sense to you, despite all the risks. If you don't know where that is, it's quite possible that you're, consciously or subconsciously, focusing primarily on the discomfort in your landscape, wishing it would just go away. I'm here to tell you that the edge you feel offers much more than just anxiety. It actually tells you loud and clear where your arena is. Now it's up to you to claim it.

Your arena is your commitment to something greater than yourself and your circumstances. While walking on the edge in your landscape for change, filled with world paradoxes, broken workplace ideas and misconceptions, as well as the pressures of your personal stories, somewhere amidst the noise, you'll discern the voice, the signal that clearly states: 'I'm going to do something about this!' This is your own sense of agency speaking.

Claiming your arena is like throwing a pebble into a pond. The pond is your landscape for change, your wider circle of impact. The pebble that you're going to throw in a particular spot in that pond is the change that you're bringing to your arena, your specific circle of influence. When you know your arena and bring your bold agency to it, you create ripples that have the power to change your whole landscape and beyond.

Considering the difference you want to make as a leader, you might rephrase the earlier question to: 'What is the pebble I want to throw, where exactly in my pond and why?' Let me tell you how it works.

There's a lot in my pond. Simply consider all the aspects of my leadership landscape: motherhood, step-motherhood, marriage, wider family, business, professional industry and community, friendship, justice, women's leadership, Europe, not to mention all the intersectionality of the identities deriving from these aspects. There's a lot in my landscape, as there is in yours.

My pebbles are the conversations that I bring to predominantly organisational leaders in my landscape. I create and engage in meaningful conversations with them, aiming to elevate their leadership consciousness and potential. There's a prerequisite in the world for developing bold leadership cultures that can radically shape our present and our future. I see this as an opportunity to better our world, one I can do something about. It's really as simple and as difficult as that.

What I see in our context of both world and workplace, and what I have experienced in my leadership landscape, has made me strongly believe that true boldness is often wasted because of our underdeveloped consciousness, our limited awareness. This leads to a misuse of power by some instead of leading to the empowerment of everyone. It goes against our birthright of integrity and ultimately freedom.

I have made it my mission to create spaces – my arenas – where I can support human transformation for the sake of a different scenario. These aren't just physical spaces such as organisational settings, but also moments in time, opportunities I seize to engage and influence. I'm not talking only about courtrooms or scheduled business events either. My books are my arenas as well, helping me enter into conversation with so many leaders out there, including you. My presence anywhere has the potential to turn into my arena. I am committed to transforming every interaction, every message, every moment into a chance to create the change I want to see to the best of my conscious abilities and my vision.

Here's what has helped me gain clarity around claiming my arena. It would be easier to give way to a natural human inclination to seek emotional relief while my reality feels on the edge, yet I've experienced that there is something crucial that we can become aware of while staying with the discomfort there. This is our fundamental choice.

I prefer the concept of knowing I can have fundamental choice over having a purpose, because for me, it already holds the power of agency by being a choice. This is how management consultant Robert

Fritz defines fundamental choice in his book *The Path of Least Resistance*: '...a choice in which you commit yourself to a basic life-orientation or a basic state of being', and then he explains, 'Once the fundamental choice is made, an entirely new basis for dealing with reality becomes available.'[43]

Having a fundamental choice elevates something other than discomfort to a high priority, transforming the edge into an opportunity for making a difference. At the core, it boils down to a few critical questions:

• What are you really ready to choose?

• What is your hope, your deepest desire for your world?

• Because of that, what emerges for you as a priority in your landscape?

Becoming conscious of the answers to these questions, you hold the transformative power to turn any edge into an opportunity. In fact, walking on your edge, you start seeing possibilities everywhere you look.

If you miss the chance to bring this choice to your awareness, any edge you walk on will – as Carl Jung is rumoured to have said – 'direct your life and you will call it fate'. It may be another restructuring project, another bad boss, another big ruthless system, another family issue or health condition, any number of conflicts of different types and sizes – any challenge in your direct landscape reflected from the world, workplace or your more intimate reality.

My fundamental choice is freedom, defined by my boldness in the face of any power, prioritising integrity over conformity. Freedom through empowerment of self and others. Understanding this might shed more light on my thirteen-year walk on the edge described earlier, but don't think that my fundamental choice is any less vital in my current arena. Working with organisational leaders to develop their consciousness is a context where resistance is frequent, as is exerting power over others.

Actually being a commitment to my fundamental choice keeps me true to my path for the sake of the change I want to see, preventing me from straying. Here's a simplistic image of this. In my business, I won't offer a development programme that compromises my beliefs about what true leadership entails. In my personal life, I won't settle for any trade off of my integrity for the temporary comfort of easing the challenges, especially since I am very much consciously choosing not to do that based on my fundamental choice.

As much as it feels difficult at moments, it really is this straightforward. Fritz explains so clearly this empowering impact of our fundamental choice: 'The meaning of human endeavour changes from actions taken in an attempt to regain emotional stability to actions taken to bring into the world the full realisation of the vision you hold.'[44]

That has shaped me and it continues to do so. The edge you walk on will gradually shape the identity you become. When you look at the world through the eyes of your fundamental choice, all you see is your work to be done, regardless of the edge you'll have to walk on to do it. When you take on that work, deciding to commit to doing something about it, all you feel is your growing self – the one with the power of agency, the bold in action – even when others looking at you fail to rationalise it and wonder out loud why you're being so irrational.

What comes to my mind is *Queen of the Desert*, a biographical drama that tells the story of Gertrude Bell, exploring her adventures in the Middle East.[45] Gertrude Bell was a writer, traveller, political officer and archaeologist who played a significant role in British imperial policy in that region during and after World War I. Best known for her influential work in what is now Iraq, she was heavily involved in the political reconfiguration of the Middle East after the fall of the Ottoman Empire.

In one of the scenes, when Sir Mark Sykes, a British diplomat and politician, challenges the independences of her motives, questioning what attracts her to the Bedouins, Bell explains that it is something beyond his and his surroundings' understanding – their freedom. She continues, 'It's their dignity. It's their poetry of life.'

Regardless of how poetic you choose to be about life, with clarity on your fundamental choice, any edge becomes a nursery of impulses informing you about your arena. Other people or events become largely irrelevant to your decision to continually put yourself on the line, walking on the edge while taking a stand for what deeply matters to you. The secret of any edge you walk along is to listen to its voice while letting go of the story so that you can hear the message it holds for you. I'm not trying to oversimplify external circumstances; rather, I aim to clarify the power of your innate boldness when activated.

Consider stepping back from my story to observe your own landscape. What can you hear through the noise of your discomfort? What is there that you are ready to do something about and why? Where will you lead the change that you crave to see and be? What is the arena that you're claiming right now? Although you may identify multiple arenas for change, perhaps simultaneously, it is crucial to claim at least one and activate your agency.

The thing is, what you care about often feels irrational for this world, and so places you on the edge, making your arena a risky spot. However, when you channel your boldness into action, this edge transforms into a space of possibilities. By its nature, the edge is not where your power stops; rather, it's where your agency begins, but that's only true if you are ready to wholeheartedly claim your arena.

On the edge of possibilities

Let me quote Bob Anderson from Leadership Circle® once again: 'Leaders must simultaneously stand for what they know and be open to the evolution of their understanding.'[46]

One of the boldest evolutions of my understanding was embracing the perspective that allows me to create from the paradox of the world, brokenness of the workplace and my walk on the edge. This taught me that the landscape in which I lead is abundant with possibilities. These possibilities exist not despite my world being on the edge, but *because* of it.

Walking on the edge, I'm exposed to countless possibilities, as long as I choose to see them. All I have to do is listen to the signals for the change that I want to happen and trust that I'm the right person to lead that change in my own personal leadership authority. Being the right person to lead, of course, involves many nuances, but someone always has to take a stand. You are not a leader at all if you never do so.

Possibilities are everywhere you look unless you're waiting for someone else to mend the broken world first. Whatever paradox and brokenness your landscape reflects, it communicates to you the critical change you passionately care about, the fundamental choice that directs you in claiming your arena and bringing your agency. If you are unable to hear that voice, you need to start by doing what we always do when there seem to be no solutions on the horizon – learn to look for them in another way, learn to listen differently. Learn more and make everyone your teacher. This will bring you clarity about the expectations your bolder self has of you.

The world on the edge, the broken workplace, your landscape at the brink – they all send a clear message to you as a leader. This message will never suggest that you take a back seat and relax, waiting for relief before you can lead effectively. Instead, it calls you to step forward now and ask yourself:

- What do I care about?
- What is mine to do?
- Where and when will I act boldly?

This urgency in leadership – the need to take immediate action and connect with our deepest passions and responsibilities – is reflected in Naomi Shihab Nye's poem *Missing the Boat*.[47] In it, she describes a moment when the boat drifts away, fading into the distance, and only then do we realise our long-standing love for the sea. Our entire context is highly informative and the edge we may be walking on is even more revealing. Our fixation on the wrong impulses, such as fear, discomfort, attachment to our sense of safety and security, can blind us to the full range of possibilities in our landscape for change, defining our missed potential in the most disappointing terms.

We have now clarified the overall leadership context through three lenses, all the way up to our own circle of impact – our leadership landscape for change. What we need to do next is explore our ways of being within it. Many of these ways of being in our landscape keep our leadership waiting at the edge and block our agency. Let's explore these ways of being first, and then we'll explore alternatives that can empower our boldness in action and support our daring walk on the edge.

KEY IDEAS

- Leadership begins in your landscape, shaped by global events, workplace trends and personal realities – your starting point for leading meaningful change.

- Constant transformation is the new normal, demanding proactive leadership.

- Your arena is the space where bold leadership comes to life, turning discomfort into agency and creating ripples of impact.

- Anchoring your leadership in a fundamental choice – a core commitment to a value, vision or longing – offers clarity and focus for bold action.

- Walking on the edge of risk and uncertainty reveals opportunities to act boldly and make an impact.

Your mirror moment

After reading this chapter, I want you to listen inward right now. Really listen and decide how you'll start leading on the edge in your own landscape – not tomorrow or the next day when resistance might cause you to miss the momentum, but in this very moment. Then, challenge yourself with these questions:

1. In your leadership landscape, what change do you feel most compelled to create? Do you trust yourself to lead this change? Are you ready to fall in love with it? How would that make a difference?

2. Think of your personal story or challenging experience. How can you use it to lead meaningful change beyond your own situation? What discomforts might this awaken and how could facing them unlock new possibilities for the change you'd love to see?

3. What is your specific circle of influence – your arena – where you feel called to act? What are the risks? Are you ready to claim that space anyway? What fundamental choice is guiding your decision?

4. What do you need to dare to do now so you don't miss the boat?

Your activation zone

- List your top three game-changing ideas from Part 1.

- Where, how and when will you apply these ideas?

- What will happen if you don't take action?

PART 2
LEADERSHIP ON THE EDGE

'At the core, we are the problem,' says Erik Fernholm, a Swedish thought leader and social entrepreneur with a background in cognitive neuroscience.[48] Fernholm, known for his dedication to promoting inner development as a foundation for personal and societal transformation, speaks about the root cause of leadership being on the edge, facing a fractured world full of crises and immense pressures: the way we approach problem solving is, in fact, the problem itself.

The challenges we face on a global scale – whether in the economy, technology, social movements or environmental stability – are deeply intertwined with our approach to solving problems. Furthermore, the global shifts disrupt our workplaces and compel us to question the sustainability of our current world of work. The collective turbulence shapes our leadership landscape, making it far from idyllic.

What does that leave us with? We find ourselves caught between the comfort of autopilot and the daring opportunity to lead on the edge. Which path will you choose? Will you succumb to the predictable yet profoundly disappointing choice of mediocrity, wasting your potential for boldness? To rise to the challenge and lead on the edge, it's imperative that you begin right now to explore what lies beneath the surface – your way of being as a leader.

Fernholm's perspective is influenced by many mentors, including Tomas Björkman, an applied philosopher and social entrepreneur. While Fernholm identifies the problem, Björkman offers a solution: 'Being human has many dimensions, and the dimension that we have been very good at exploring during the last couple of 100 years has been the external world, but we have come to a point where the outside perspective has to be complemented by an inside perspective.'[49]

Fernholm and Björkman are just two of the many researchers, professors, thought leaders and practitioners from various fields who are part of the Inner

Development Goals (IDG) non-profit initiative, which seeks to bring the power of inner development to better respond to the global challenges humanity faces today.[50] This initiative emerged in response to the slow progress towards the United Nations' Sustainable Development Goals (SDGs), adopted in 2015.[51] In essence, the initiative is aiming to address our limited internal capacity to respond to the complex challenges in an ever-changing world by offering the transformation skills we need to learn individually and collectively.

As the IDG initiative states, the primary force behind creating a sustainable world is us – human beings. Everyone, regardless of their field or sphere of influence, must embark on a journey of learning in which exploring our inner world becomes part of our personal curriculum. If this initiative seems too broad for your leadership landscape, let me clarify the connection: this conversation ultimately comes down to how we as leaders respond to challenges within our own circle of impact and influence. Our responses either perpetuate mediocrity or create bold, meaningful change.

Regardless of what your leadership landscape looks like, you face a critical choice: remain waiting at the edge in your comfort zone, or continue walking on the edge, embracing risk and change. The coming chapters will explore patterns associated with both choices. The choice that transcends mediocrity requires a shift in perspective, cultivating vision, passion and grit, and redefining how you as a leader engage with emotions, power and change.

This section of the book looks into how that choice involves embodying dual somewhat paradoxical identities – being both stoic and vulnerable, autonomous yet dependent, ambitious while humble – and calibrating these traits as needed. Before rushing ahead, though, we'll explore what it means to wait at the edge – what patterns bring us there, what we believe we gain from it, and how this contrasts with the true essence of leading on the edge in extraordinary ways.

Both our world and our leadership on the edge start with the way we, as leaders and human beings, choose to be. Our development, and thus our ability to create better solutions, begins by exploring these ways of being, focusing on our mindset, life stance and character. That's precisely what we'll explore first before diving into action, to prepare ourselves for the extraordinary opportunity of leading on the edge.

FOUR

Waiting At The Edge

Waiting at the edge might feel like a comfort zone, but there's nothing truly comfortable about it. Rather than offering genuine comfort, it's an area of tolerable risk where we believe our breaking point won't be tested. Put differently, we wait there to manage our deepest fears. There might be a lot of action, but without real conscious and bold agency, the risks we take are minimised – if they exist at all. We remain waiting, stuck at the edge, focusing primarily on the emotional relief this choice brings because it feels safer than moving forward.

Earlier, I challenged you to consider whether you view your work as more than just something that gives you a sense of safety, a source of existential security. Now I want to remind you of how we are wired as human beings through the message commonly attributed to Abraham Maslow, which suggests that we are constantly faced with two choices: to step forward into growth or to step back into safety. I want to make it clear that what I call 'waiting at the edge' is essentially a step back from the edge and a hesitation to fully dare to step on to it – in other words, it's a retreat into safety.

As we step back into safety, waiting at the edge, we often find ourselves believing in one of three key stories: 'I can't do anything about it'; 'I must do everything about it'; 'I don't want to do anything about it'. These stories correspond to three recurring patterns I've observed in my work with leaders: the overwhelming world, the hero's martyrdom and the self(ish)-care pandemic.

Each pattern reveals not only what it looks like when leaders wait at the edge, but also the type of culture they create. We'll explore how merely waiting at the edge can cultivate a culture overwhelmed by challenges rather than empowered to overcome them, marked by indifference rather than care and characterised by separation rather than ownership.

Let's not wait. It's time to go deeper into these patterns.

Overwhelming world

One of the ways of waiting at the edge is experiencing what I call the 'overwhelming world'. I'm sure we've all had our moments of feeling overwhelmed and, as a result, being passive. Our emotional reaction to the latest news, ongoing wars, societal conflicts, environmental crises, organisational changes and personal challenges believes in a story that whispers, 'This reality is too big for me.' In other words – I can't do anything about it.

I run a boutique leadership development consultancy called Bold Leadership Culture and in our programmes portfolio, my team and I use the Leadership Circle Profile® (LCP®).[52] We consider it a powerful philosophy that serves as your mirror, uncovering your ways of being in your landscape for change. LCP® helps you understand your underdeveloped leadership identity leading to your underutilised leadership potential.

One of the ways LCP® does that is to uncover your three major reactive tendencies: complying, protecting and controlling.[53] The complying dimension measures the extent to which you derive a sense of self-worth and security by complying with the expectations of others rather than acting on your own intentions and desires. The protecting dimension evaluates the belief that you can safeguard yourself and establish self-worth by withdrawing – staying distant, hidden, aloof, cynical, superior or overly rational. The controlling dimension assesses how much you derive a sense of security and self-worth from task accomplishment, personal achievement and power.

Each of these three key dimensions includes specific tendencies within it. Complying consists of being conservative, pleasing, belonging and being passive. Protecting includes being distant, critical and arrogant. Controlling involves being autocratic, ambitious, driven and perfect. In this chapter, I will focus on the tendencies I see as closely tied to the patterns of waiting at the edge – specifically passivity, drive and distance.

Passivity measures the extent to which you give your power away to others and to external circumstances. In the passive tendency, you're simply being inactive in your leadership landscape. You surrender in ways and places you shouldn't be doing so. When I'm coaching leaders who are scoring highly in the passive tendency, I notice their deep-seated belief that their efforts have no impact.

Such leaders feel a sense of powerlessness to create their desired future. In fact, they see vision as something that belongs to others, not to them. In the context of the overwhelming world, instead of focusing on their vision, they are allowing themselves to be focused on their internal emotional landscape – their feeling of overwhelm. They're being guided by a self-protecting belief that aims to offer comfort: 'It's bigger than me, so I need to switch off.'

We cannot blame them. In the wider world, there is an extreme perspective, a seductive invitation to over-indulge in comfort, but comfort and vision rarely go together. Read that again:

Comfort and vision do not go hand in hand.

Comfort is contrary to the idea of being human and finding meaning in growth, yet our modern world seems designed to maximise convenience, minimise effort and offer instant gratification. Educational paradigms of my childhood championed the virtues of hard work, patience and enduring discomfort for long-term goals. The message was clear: 'If you want to achieve something, be prepared to work hard and face obstacles along the way.' Today, the dominant narrative – supported by powerful social media and reinforced by overprotective caregivers in all their good intentions – sounds different. It promises a world where anything is achievable without pain or effort: 'You are bigger than anything. You can have all you want without tolerating what you dislike.'

This appealing but misleading message discourages us from stepping out of our comfort zone to walk on the edge. Instead, it advises waiting at the edge until we have found comfort, but prioritising comfort over taking a leap forward undermines growth and ultimately leads to crises of meaning. As we avoid challenges, we diminish our potential for impact, and that eventually feels everything but comfortable.

In a context where comfort is king, it's no wonder that the world on the edge leaves us feeling overwhelmed. There is a different way, though: we could be using our emotional discomfort as the fuel to grow and create change. Missing the chance to do so, we'll often find ourselves shut down by discomfort, paralysed instead of empowered by the potential it holds.

This is how in today's leadership, the culture of over-whelm buries the potential for a culture of empower-ment. We wait at the edge, giving our power away to a world that feels too much for us, and end up switching off, shrinking within its overwhelm-ing grip, feeling powerless and finding comfort in our passivity.

If you're wondering how this plays out in an organ-isational setting, take an extreme although not unreal-istic example of being handed another restructuring project – your fifth in as many years – to 'optimise' what you and those you lead believe is an already effi-cient system. What might you see on some of your colleagues' faces, and your own, as you invite every-one for yet another round of changes?

Hero's martyrdom

Previously, in discussing our broken workplace, I highlighted the common trend of spending exces-sive hours at work. Now I want to explore how busy-ness is yet another way of waiting at the edge, caught in what I call 'hero's martyrdom' where we believe we must do everything about every single thing.

Warren Buffet is often quoted as saying busy is the new stupid. I'll admit, part of me still struggles to fully embrace this idea, yet I recognise that busyness, far from being a badge of honour, often leads to a sense of depletion, ultimately nurturing indifference as a coping mechanism.

Let me explain the narrative behind this pattern. Many senior leaders I work with share their feeling of ceaseless entrapment: 'There is no escape from this prison. No matter how fast I am, it keeps outpacing me. It will never end.' These leaders, perpetually busy, struggle to discern the true essence of their work (not their job, their *work*). Caught in a relentless cycle, they remain at the edge, waiting there for years.

Because they're in a state of continuous motion, it may not feel like they're waiting. In fact, for them it probably feels like anything but waiting. In reality, though, they're not moving towards their most meaningful goals, most likely because they don't truly know what they are.

The key missing element is genuine presence with themselves, others and their work day in and day out – a deeper awareness of their identity and their purpose. Many will argue that, given the relentless pace and pressures of our workplace today, falling into this trap is all too easy, but it is a great recipe for feeling deeply passionless until we totally burn out.

In the LCP® assessments, many of these leaders score highly in the driven tendency – a constant state of pushing, avoiding the present moment. Being driven can also be a form of 'power over' that involves making decisions for others. This may come from the good intention of helping everyone, yet it means these leaders are not fully trusting anyone. This tendency can be an urgent, frequently subconscious, need to rescue and be a hero leader.

Paradoxically, these hero leaders/rescuers are reluctant to question or challenge the root cause of the status quo and bring true change within their leadership landscape. As a result, they haven't got an arena to claim. On one hand, they are exerting power over others by executing tasks; on the other, they give their power away in failing to honour their true purpose. While action dominates, without utilising the 'pause' button to get fully present with their inner and outer landscape, these leaders lose their agency – their ability to act from a place of genuine purposeful power and clarity.

This drive tendency can be so intense with its underlying subconscious need for heroism that instead of creating a culture of care, it ironically creates a culture of indifference disguised in narratives like the ones I've heard many times from my clients: 'Just keep on going forward. The pace can't be slowed down or stopped, so keep pushing through.' In this culture, there's nothing pulling these leaders in the sense of them feeling truly alive and connected to what they deeply care about, to the meaningful change that matters to them.

The driven tendency serves as a warning against constantly being in push mode, which is a common scenario in many organisations where too many leaders do too much, losing focus on the most strategic ways to add value and make a difference. In hero's martyrdom, leaders eventually cultivate indifference as a coping mechanism, with everything and nothing too often being equally important.

Self(ish)-care pandemic

There's a saying that reminds us that self-care is a critical component of sustainable leadership: 'You cannot pour from an empty cup.' Loving ourselves and filling our cup is essential. We need to be well to be able to be of service to others and the change we seek to create.

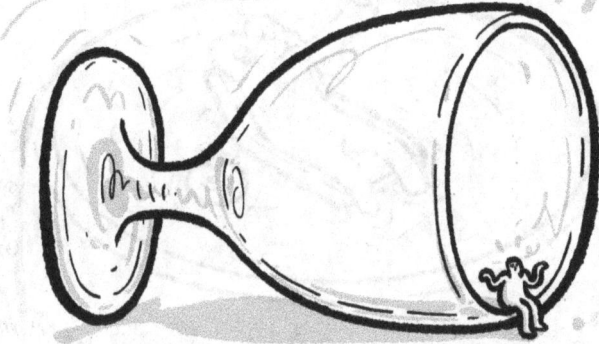

However, when we prioritise ourselves to an excessive, almost obsessive level in a landscape that calls for our leadership, we risk falling into what I call the 'self(ish)-care pandemic' pattern. This mindset often sounds like, 'I don't want to do anything about it!' It's a resistance to taking action unless it puts oneself first.

What I'm referring to here are misconceptions of true, authentic self-care. Scroll through social media and you'll see narratives championing self-care to the point where it overshadows everything else: 'Put yourself first, always. Everyone else can wait'; 'Your comfort is your right; never sacrifice it for anyone'; 'If it doesn't serve you, leave it. Your happiness is what matters most'; 'Check with yourself daily to see what you need and make sure you get it'. Put them all together and they carry a screaming message: 'My needs first. Me, me, me.'

Stay with these perspectives for a moment. While they may sound empowering on the surface, they subtly promote a form of dominance – the choice to prioritise oneself above all else, to the detriment of what could be our unique service to the world. True self-care is never (ab)used as a way out of our sense of ownership for the world around us.

Pursuing self-care in this way can create a gap, distancing us from our potential contributions to the world. It's like retreating from our leadership landscape into a self-created microcosm – a necessary place for recovery, but once recovered, we should return and continue walking on the edge. However, if we stay withdrawn, the risk is that we fall into a form of avoidance, becoming distant and isolated. This distance is a reactive tendency, as seen in the LCP®, where we wait at the edge instead of walking on it.

In the late summer of 2022, I attended the first European Gathering of Leadership Circle® Practitioners, held in Uslar, Germany. Located in nature, away from the world's bustle, the venue was a paradise of tranquillity. A spacious room with its wooden architecture and high ceilings created an inviting atmosphere for almost fifty people, including myself.

The late Liberto Pereda, then managing director of Leadership Circle® Europe, masterfully led our session. Under his guidance, we were placed under pressure in an experiential exercise designed to reveal our reactions to a high level of discomfort. My reaction led me to distance – a measure of my tendency to establish a sense of personal worth and security through withdrawal, being superior and remaining aloof, emotionally closed off and above it all. Being distant, we withdraw from leadership opportunities that require our active presence and participation.

During that experience, I realised that distance is a form of exercising 'power over'. For years, distance had been my primary reactive tendency in stressful situations. I would withdraw to take care of myself, especially when walking on the edge felt too challenging. I chose to rise above it all, separate myself from everyone and everything.

Stepping into this space for recovery isn't inherently problematic – it's disconnecting and remaining there that's concerning. If we do so for too long, we as leaders feel a lack of ability to effect change and make a difference to the way things are. This is just another way to say that we are giving up our agency.

The idea of authentic self-care is not to create a culture of separation in which everyone remains distant and retreated, prioritising self above all else. On the contrary, when practised sincerely, self-care supports the culture of ownership, preparing us to engage more actively with the world around us after we have taken a breath to recover. To avoid falling into the trap of the self(ish)-care pandemic, we must have an element of service – a conscious practice where we nurture ourselves not just for our own benefit, but to be able to continue to walk on the edge, knowing our arena and the agency we bring to it.

In his book *The Wealth Money Can't Buy*, Robin Sharma says it perfectly: 'Don't let self-care ruin your self-worth.'[54] There are many leaders out there using their inner work as an excuse to avoid facing fears and taking actions that will, as Sharma says, 'make their genius real'.

Good self-care needs to be a top priority as our best life will be a direct reflection of our inner wellbeing. Sharma invites us to 'balance this with the ongoing building of a base of supreme self-worth, born of elite performance, extraordinary achievement, and the consistent making of outright masterpieces'. You have every potential to do this, and even a responsibility towards the world, but none of it can happen unless you continue your committed walk on the edge, even while taking self-recovery breaks.

The deal on the edge

Earlier, I explained that waiting at the edge means a retreat into safety, avoiding risk and focusing on the emotional relief this choice brings. Additionally, I explored three related patterns or ways of being: passively surrendering our power to the overwhelming world; being driven, caught in the paradox of taking power over others while simultaneously giving it away in hero's martyrdom; and remaining distant, claiming hidden dominance in the self(ish)-care pandemic.

These are not the only ways of waiting at the edge, but they have emerged as predominant patterns among the leaders I've worked with over the past decade. I'm sure in real life, we can all creatively identify additional versions of these three.

It's important to visualise what waiting at the edge versus walking on the edge looks like. To me, it's standing on an actual physical cliff edge where the earth drops down into the sea. Even if you haven't visited such a place, I'm sure you can imagine somewhere where the mainland meets the water.

Twenty years ago, I discovered Cabo da Roca, Portugal's westernmost point where the relentless Atlantic Ocean waves crash against towering cliffs, offering stunning beauty. Ever since then, I've considered it more than a geographical location. It is a metaphorical frontier, a place where the solid earth daringly confronts the vast untamed sea. Even today, I feel my walk there was more than a mere physical activity; rather than a casual stroll along a cliff, it was a deep introspection along the very brink of the world.

There, on the edge, every step is a delicate dance between risk and safety, between the known and the unknown. It is a place where the whisper of the wind carries more than just the salt of the sea; it carries the stories of ages, the silent songs of explorers and dreamers who have stood at this very brink. Just by standing here, you join this invisible fellowship, connected through time and space by the shared experience of confronting the unknown, the yet to be explored and – only potentially – understood.

Even though there is a touristic hustle at Cabo da Roca, in which one can easily be distracted by the crowds flocking to souvenir shops or indulging in refreshments, there lies a deeper experience. If you can anchor yourself in your own presence in the middle of nature's magnificence, the edge in its physical appearance becomes a mirror reflecting your innermost thoughts, fears and aspirations.

The edge, therefore, isn't just a physical spot; it's a state of mind. It invites you to realise that stepping forward to the edge in your leadership is so much more than moving physically. Walking instead of waiting is a conscious step towards deep understanding of yourself and your work in the world.

If you're anything like me, at Cabo da Roca, you might feel the fear of falling as you approach the edge. I've personally experienced how this fear can keep one physically motionless, even while one's mind races at 100 miles an hour. At the edge, looking straight ahead, it feels like there's nowhere to go, but that's only one way to see reality. What if you simply turn your head to the left or right? By doing so, you realise there's a path along which you can walk. It's still risky, but instead of feeling stuck at the edge with no options, you shift your perspective, which suddenly expands the landscape of possibilities.

You see, often, we aren't really stuck – we're just stubborn. Waiting at the edge looks far less comfortable than it actually is, and yet we're attached to it. Daring to walk on the edge towards what we deeply care about is what brings true discomfort.

We always have the choice to walk on the edge, transforming both ourselves and the world around us. The power to claim our arena and create change is in our hands, but as marketing expert Seth Godin points out, it's 'tempting to imagine we have less power than we do. It lets us off the hook'.[55] This self-deception is just another story we tell ourselves to justify our patterns of waiting at the edge. It's a way of simply being mediocre.

Waiting at the edge, we hold on to a narrative about what we must do to preserve our sense of security. This narrative encourages us to keep playing small, pushing us to manipulate external circumstances to restore a feeling of safety on the inside. That internal voice can become so dominant that it shapes our lives and decisions, often diverting us from the changes we truly want to create. Eventually, it corners our sense of agency until we finally give up.

Ever wonder how people sabotage their potential? They prioritise safety instead. In their white paper *Reactive to Creative Leadership*, Bob Anderson and Bill Adams warn us that in case we choose to orient on whatever wants to express itself with our lives, we live into the futures we were actually born to create: '...we accept the inherent risk of leading, of living full-out, and that brings with it a sense of security. To lead is to live at the edge.'[56] If you're not up for this deal, you may never get to experience a sense of inner security. You might still take many actions that seem reasonable for building your sense of security in the outer world, but you'll make little progress that is truly meaningful for you.

The deal is not simply to be, but to become. Becoming requires uncomfortable walks along the risky edge. If we only subscribe to a tolerable level of discomfort, we won't grow, nor will we contribute to our world. We won't truly live, let alone lead.

What if you're someone who's rarely felt unsafe, born into a life of comfort and predictability? The truth is, while our outward image may appear secure, the internal sense of risk is deeply personal for each of us. Even those with seemingly comfortable lives must confront their own inner boundaries of discomfort to grow. When I speak to corporate leaders in Eastern Europe about change, the message of leaving their comfort zone and taking risks can resonate differently to leaders in Western Europe, which is why it must be offered from a tailored perspective.

No matter how much safety and comfort you've experienced, there's one question you can ask yourself: what gives you anxiety and an almost unbearable sense of ambiguity? You'll know the answer. Staying with that answer for a while holds the key to understanding what your walk on the edge might be.

I love how James Hollis, the author of *Finding Meaning in the Second Half of Life*, puts it: 'Psychological, spiritual, or leadership development always requires a greater capacity in us for tolerating anxiety and ambiguity. The ability to accept this troubled state, endure it, and commit to life is the moral measure of our maturity.'[57]

What a wonderful way to describe the walk on the edge, but what a disheartening truth it is to realise that not all leaders are ripe and ready, regardless of how secure they may appear.

KEY IDEAS

- Waiting at the edge means staying in a safe risk zone, seeking comfort instead of stepping into bold action.
- There are three patterns of waiting at the edge:
  - **Overwhelming world**: you retreat into passivity, feeling powerless and giving up your vision to external circumstances.
  - **Hero's martyrdom**: you retreat into drive, taking on too much, losing focus on what truly matters.
  - **Self(ish)-care pandemic**: you retreat into distance, applying misguided self-care that leads to withdrawal and neglect of leadership responsibilities.
- The deal in leadership is to live on the edge, embrace risks and create meaningful change while discovering true inner security.

Your mirror moment

Nothing creates change as instantly as moments of truth – when you dare to engage deeply, exposed with nowhere to hide. Face the moment of truth now and ask yourself:

1. When it feels unsafe, do you retreat into passivity, drive or distance?

2. What excuses do you use to stay there, waiting at the edge? How are these excuses preventing you from creating real change?

3. What risky action would transform you into a different leader?

Then, ask these questions of those you believe are ripe and ready to join you in the leadership conversation:

1. Are you ready to accept the deal of living and leading on the edge? What would that look like for you? For your wider system? What are the risks? What could be the rewards?

2. Are you settling for mediocrity by waiting at the edge? What bold move could you make today to change that?

3. How would that change you, your team and your organisational culture? How could that help to change the world?

FIVE
Walking On The Edge

Here's a crucial question: if waiting at the edge is your comfort zone, why would you choose to shift your view, leave that spot and start walking along the risky line? Furthermore, why should anyone follow you?

The late Gareth Jones and his co-author Robert Goffee posed a similarly provocative question in their McKinsey award-winning *Harvard Business Review* article, which later became a bestselling book, 'Why should anyone be led by you?'[58] They experienced how this question typically silences a room of executives, leaving nothing but the sound of knees knocking.

Regardless of whether these questions have just silenced you or not, consider the leadership insights

of Simon Sinek—a motivational speaker and organisational consultant—who champions the idea that true leadership emerges when our actions inspire others to dream, learn, do and become more. Now reflect on the three patterns of waiting at the edge: being passive in the overwhelming world; being driven in hero's martyrdom; and being distant in the self(ish)-care pandemic. How much do any of these patterns truly inspire others to dream, learn, do and become more? While I don't subscribe to a strict black-or-white view of leadership, I suspect we'd agree the answer is not much.

What's a different way of being a leader? Once you shift your view from the edge, where do you start?

There are three essential cornerstones to leading on the edge: personal leadership vision, passion and grit. Each in its own way offers a response to the distinct patterns of merely waiting at the edge: personal vision addresses passivity within the overwhelming world; passion counters the drive within hero's martyrdom; and grit mitigates the distance of the self(ish)-care pandemic. While these responses may appear linear for the sake of learning, in reality, leadership is rarely this straightforward; rather, it's shaped by the complexities of both our landscape and our human nature.

Personal leadership vision

Leadership is being visionary. SD Friedman, an organisational psychologist and co-author of *Parents Who Lead*,[59] speaks of a personal leadership vision and defines it as 'a compelling image of an achievable future'.[60] According to Friedman, it's crucial for focusing on what you deeply care about: the change you seek to create and the identity you aspire to become as you act on that change.

If you have this vision, you must know that it's deeply rooted in your past experiences, clearly looks into the future and speaks to circumstances in your current leadership landscape. It embodies who you are and what you stand for, mobilising both you and those you lead to work together towards a change in the future that you all want to see.

Doesn't that sound wonderful and inspiring? What gets in the way for so many leaders out there? Why aren't we seeing more visionary leadership?

Understanding what having a vision really means creates the biggest issue. Hear this: having a vision means being bold and committed enough to deeply care about something with such conviction that you declare it as a future reality. This means you're making present decisions with the confidence that the future is certain.

It's challenging in the extreme to hold a vision for the future while trying to maintain a sense of security in the present. You are taking risks now for the sake of something that may never happen. This requires bringing your agency to your arena in the present for what is yet to come and is therefore unknown.

It's difficult to maintain a vision while being afraid of the unknown. It might seem easier – and arguably cleverer – to give in to passivity in your overwhelming present world to stay safe.

This brings to mind the loving but limiting way I was raised – you probably got a hint of it if you've read my book *Bold Reinvented*.[61] 'Whatever you do, please – just be clever' – I can still hear my mother's well-intentioned words resounding in my ears like a life-limiting mantra that shaped my character for almost forty years. It was a refrain that would echo in my mind many times a day, especially in moments when I stood at the crossroads of important decisions. This was my mother's version of 'stay safe' and it crept into my brain like a thief, influencing my perception of the world, making me excessively cautious. Knowing the remarkably bold actions my mother took in her life, I realise this must have been contrary to her deeply caring intentions.

In my young adulthood, these words were my constant background noise. They acted as an anxiety, defining my attitude towards my choices. I got to associate safety with cleverness, making sure I always chose the 'clever' path, although I often ended up choosing none for fear of making mistakes.

At the same time, I felt strongly that a world of possibilities existed beyond the realm of being clever and staying safe. However, I did not dare to hold that vision, until setbacks, development and time finally replaced 'stay safe' with 'what's worth the risk of walking on the edge?'

With a little bit of practice of taking risks, you simply get to know that – in the courageous walk in the middle of the unknown – the self you're evolving into will unfailingly catch you every time you fall. The more you practise risk-taking, the more you trust this outcome.

There's another important message I'd like to share regarding the idea of a personal leadership vision. Although the term itself implies 'personal', we can sometimes fall into the trap of being influenced by general beliefs, common notions of success or stories of how our vision 'should' look.

What, in that case, makes for a good vision? Let me share a personal story to illustrate what I mean.

Because my business experienced significant growth in 2023, I decided to quickly expand the Bold Leadership Culture team at the start of 2024. My vision was to build an organisation inspired by other consultancies within my network that I saw as examples of success, but although I continued along that path, something didn't feel quite right.

In March 2024, a serendipitous moment occurred when I received an invitation from my friend Günter Westphal.[62] Günter, with whom I share a passion for personal and leadership transformation, asked me to join him as a participant in a programme called the Leadership Development Intensive (LDI) in Munich. Despite the timing being inconvenient and thinking it wasn't what I needed, I felt something within me urge me to accept.

The programme was originally created by Dr John J Scherer, who famously said, 'As a leader and a human being, you don't have to change yourself; you have to come home to yourself. That changes everything.'[63] He is absolutely right. After four intensive days, I felt as though I had truly come home to myself.

At a profound level, a clarity emerged regarding my personal leadership vision. In the programme, this is referred to as your greater purpose statement (GPS). It's yours and yours alone. No external notion of what constitutes a 'successful' vision can shape it. That's simply how you play it safe.

I understood this intellectually; indeed, it's something I teach, yet when it comes to ourselves, sometimes we need a mirror held directly in front of us. For me, GPS was that mirror – a reflector where I saw my vision with complete clarity, and it was vastly different from what I'd been telling myself my vision should be.

Your personal leadership vision is the imprint of your soul. There is no blueprint for it to be found in someone else's story, nor should there be. Your uniqueness is sacred and your work is to embrace it fully.

Coming back to the overwhelming world, for your leadership to move beyond passivity and step into the boldness of walking on the edge, you must engage with your personal leadership vision in a way that defies what feels possible, clever or safe. You need to be clear: what do you stand for as a leader? What change are you determined to create? How will you take action? What's worth risking everything for? What will it cost you if you hesitate?

Are you ready to answer these questions?

Passion

Leadership is being passionate. Earlier in this book, I highlighted how in our workplaces we often prioritise a sense of security over passion. Now I want to explore the difference between passionately walking on the edge and waiting at it, simply being driven in hero's martyrdom.

Let's begin with some insights on passion. Melissa Cardon, a professor at the University of Tennessee, has been a researcher of passion for many years. To distinguish what she's talking about when she speaks about passion, she coined the term 'entrepreneurial passion', defining it as a 'positive, intense feeling about something that deeply matters to you personally'.[64] Steve Jobs claimed that those fuelled by passion can change the world for the better, precisely because passion will sustain them when challenges occur: 'You have to have a lot of passion for what you are doing because it is so hard... If you don't, any rational person would give up.'[65]

Passion is vital to leadership, yet many of my clients struggle to differentiate it from mere drive. A simple method is to examine your intentions. You cannot be walking on the edge while simultaneously anxiously protecting yourself from potential setbacks. Being driven often means relentlessly striving to avoid failure. You work tirelessly to prevent negative outcomes, but this anxious focus can push you away from the present. As a result, you may become blind to the opportunities right in front of you or avoid them altogether because they seem too risky.

Being passionate, you're open to what you most care about, regardless of the discomfort you may be experiencing. You're non-attached to the final outcome. Passion, therefore, keeps you present and aware, fully embracing the experience in both your inner and your outer world.

Drive is anxious and frenetic; passion is grounded and alert. As such, passion enables you to rise to the opportunity, which is something I'll speak more about over the coming chapters when we cover the action of risking. For now, let's stay with what passion is and what its impact may be as opposed to the one of drive.

Passion is expansive. It's a state of being that grows and intensifies over time, becoming a significant part of your continuously evolving identity. In contrast, drive can diminish you over time, leaving you small, depleted and exhausted. With passion, your spark grows. With drive, your flame eventually dies. Passion becomes clearer and more pronounced over time, illuminating your walk on the edge. On the other hand, drive can confuse you, as it often leads to you losing yourself in the relentless pursuit of external validation and the need to continuously prove your worth no matter the path.

The impact of your passion is evident in the way it draws people towards you. Passion is magnetic, attracting others with its energy. The impact of drive can push people away, as the constant pressure creates beliefs of continuous insufficiency. Passion brings clarity and enthusiasm to not only sustain you, but also inspire those around you. It is, therefore, a source of empowerment that gives you the courage to take risks.

Passion, essentially, is the antidote to fear, as it shifts your focus from what you might lose to what you stand to gain, filling your walk on the edge with meaning.

Grit

Leadership is being gritty. Passion serves as the bridge between discomfort and change, but when passion inevitably meets pain, grit becomes essential.

Angela Duckworth, a psychologist and popular science author, is best known for her research on grit. In her bestselling book *Grit*, she explores why a blend of passion and persistence, not merely talent or intelligence, is the actual secret to success.[66] Reading her book, you'll find out that if she were ever to choose a tattoo, it would be the Japanese proverb: 'Fall seven, rise eight.' What a great message for all those walking on the edge!

Here's how I understand the grit required to walk on the edge: activational hope and self-discipline. Duckworth speaks of a distinct kind of hope that gritty individuals possess – the one that has nothing to do with luck and everything to do with getting up again. This hope is reliant on the conviction that our own efforts can improve the future.

Notice the difference between this attitude and the self(ish)-care pandemic pattern of long periods of distance where leaders feel powerless to effect change. They wait at the edge, giving up on their own sense of agency. The gritty people Duckworth speaks of are all about agency. They act beyond the feeling that tomorrow will be better. Rather, they resolve to make tomorrow better, saying: 'I'm going to do something about it!'

It is exactly this resolve that indicates you are walking on the edge, feeling what I call an activational hope deep inside your bones. Activational hope is one of the key elements you need to claim your arena. The other element is self-discipline, which has been fundamental in everything I have ever created in my life and leadership.

Our commitments come to life through our self-discipline. The late Zig Ziglar, motivational speaker and inspirational author, said: 'It was character that got us out of bed, commitment that moved us into action, and discipline that enabled us to follow through.'[67] What I hear from this is that self-discipline helps us sustain what we're truly committed to.

While we can all have different definitions of self-discipline, I'd love here to reduce it down to how self-discipline really feels for me: an embodied sense of determination. Self-discipline has always focused my full attention on whatever I am committed to, sustaining my vision and passion even at moments when I do not feel like walking on the edge. Self-discipline reigns in the absence of motivation.

In essence, self-discipline prevents you from waiting until things 'feel right' before taking action. In your current leadership landscape, this could be one of the most crucial muscles to develop to walk on the edge. While the boldness to walk on the edge is innate – we are all capable of it – fully expressing this boldness will always depend on one thing: our disciplined practice.

Boldness

Boldness is a muscle to build up. One of the best ways to do this is to redefine our relationship with three critical areas: emotions, power and change. In line with that, we'll explore the three dimensions of boldness: emotional, relational and intellectual, unpacking how each of these can help us walk on the edge.

Emotional boldness

You may have heard more than once that courage is not the absence of fear. Moreover, the greater the courage, the greater the fear. If you're capable of fully embodying this mindset, you must have developed the ability to embrace contrasting emotions: fear and courage, sadness and joy, terror and excitement. This ability to be emotionally bold helps you to keep acting even when you carry a bag full of opposing emotions with you.

Psychologist and author Susan David speaks about 'bothness' – the capacity to simultaneously hold conflicting emotions: 'This bothness – the integration of all emotions into your life, even the challenging ones – is a litmus test of psychological health and wellbeing.'[68] She goes on to explain that bothness is being able to carry a difficult experience inside ourselves while making sure it doesn't define us or what we do.

Emotionally bold leaders possess a unique perspective on emotions. They skilfully navigate their own emotions while understanding and responding to those of others. They can even sense the unspoken emotions in the space around them – especially when no one is acknowledging them or, worse, everyone is trying to hide them. It's like naming the elephant in the room – something bold leaders not only see clearly, but also have the courage to reveal. They have mastered the art of normalising any emotion from themselves or others, whether it's comfortable or uncomfortable.

Normalising emotions is one of the greatest leadership abilities in today's world. It's also one of the rarest leadership skills. We often normalise situations that trigger uncomfortable emotions while suppressing the feelings themselves instead of normalising and embracing them too. I'll explore this further in Part 3.

For now, let's consider the possibilities that open up when we normalise what truly needs normalising – our emotions. This enables us to view emotions as valuable signals and sources of information, rather than as grounds for self-judgement and judging others or situations. In learning how to normalise emotions, we develop a capacity to simply sit with any emotion in complete acceptance, and that will position us as masters of the potential control emotions might have over our actions. If a certain emotion is uncomfortable, it does not mean it will take us away or discourage us from our work in any given arena.

It's impossible to walk on the edge and simultaneously protect ourselves from a full range of emotions. As Susan David says, 'There is wisdom in bothness. Bothness gives us access to the full spectrum of life.'[69] We cannot access the full spectrum of life by staying safe from the emotions that give us discomfort, those that we're most likely naming as negative. There is no such thing as a positive or negative emotion. There are only those that create comfort or discomfort for us, all of which serve as information about what matters most in any given moment.

Here's a story that illustrates how this panned out for me. In July 2023, I was diagnosed with insulin resistance and was terrified by the conversation with my physician, who warned that I could soon end up with Type 2 diabetes if I continued with my then lifestyle. I spent a good two days feeling sorry for myself, yet at the same time, I held on to hope through my determination to do something about it.

You could argue that feeling sorry for myself was how I expressed resistance to change while holding the intention of making a radical shift in my lifestyle. On a practical level, it was about admitting that it would be hard and I'd rather not be in this position, while at the same time choosing to eagerly embrace the belief that I had the resourcefulness to do something about it. It still feels like walking on the edge, but I remain self-disciplined, putting one foot in front of the other, day by day.

One day, while running on a track in the sports centre near my parents' house on the coast, I noticed the slogan of a sportswear company written on the basketball net: 'The only way is through.'[70] This phrase perfectly sums up leadership that's walking on the edge. When we're faced with the need to walk on the edge, especially one we would not have asked for, our instinct is to retreat, seek shortcuts and avoid discomfort, staying safe, secure and away from the edge. However, true progress demands that we go through the pain, discomfort, fear and range of other emotions.

In a highly disruptive landscape, emotional boldness helps us disrupt ourselves so we can self-innovate, act, create, change and lead, but this is only possible if we are committed to walking through the circumstances that part of us wishes we didn't have to. That's what emotional boldness is all about.

Relational boldness

In addition to being conscious and intentional about our relationship with emotions, walking on the edge requires us to understand our relationship with power.

Every relationship – whether it's with ourselves, others, the world, our workplace, our landscape or our arena – carries some form of power dynamics. Throughout this book, you'll frequently hear me mention the concept of power, beginning with my personal stories. Power deeply intrigues me, in part because it's essential for creating any change. Developing the ability to be conscious and intentional about power is what I call relational boldness.

To develop relational boldness, we need to understand power beyond what we have been told it is. We must acknowledge different existing dynamics of power so that we can consciously open ourselves up to its real potential. That's what power is – it's a potential – but our narrative is likely to have been shaped by power abuse. The question is, how can we shift the narrative about power or, more importantly, where do we start?

I see five essential forms of power dynamics: giving power away to others, having power over others, standing in power within oneself, having power with others and standing in power with the system. Let's start by understanding what each one means and how they are connected.

Giving power away to others is perhaps best captured in the words attributed to American novelist Alice Walker, who claimed that the most common way people give up their power is by thinking they don't have any. We often mistakenly believe we lack the power to effect change, assuming it must be someone else – someone that we perceive as more powerful than us – who will come to rescue us and take real action on the changes we wish to see. As human beings, we find all the right arguments to explain why we lack power, when in truth, we lack courage.

Let me offer a radical example of actual rescuing. During the catastrophic floods that hit Bosnia and Herzegovina in 2023, Lejla Zalihić was at home with her family when the rising waters began to consume their house.[71] Her thirteen-year-old daughter was swept away by the floodwaters, carried nearly three kilometres downstream. Without hesitation, Lejla leapt from the third floor of her family's house into the raging waters and swam those three kilometres to rescue her daughter, managing to pull her to safety despite the extreme conditions. Lejla was later hospitalised for her injuries, but her courageous act saved her daughter's life.

While you might argue that this is an example of maternal instinct refusing to give its power away, the pertinent point is that our sense of whether we possess power is shaped by our beliefs. If extreme circumstances can convince us, even momentarily, that we do have power, could other conditions do the same?

As far as **having power over others** is concerned, a clear example came with the 2024 Olympic and Paralympic Games, hosted in Paris, France. At the time, the country had banned its Muslim athletes from wearing the hijab.[72] As was rightly pointed out all over social media, this meant that Muslim women had to choose between their faith and their sport. Ironically, the mascot for the Olympic Games was Olympic Phryge, inspired by the iconic Phrygian cap, a long-standing symbol of liberty in French history. If you were to visit the official website, you'd read that the name and design had been intentionally chosen as symbols of freedom.[73] Quite a paradox given the ban.

This control and dominance is a classic example of 'having power over', which says, 'I won't allow you to be who you are, because I can...' or worse '... because I'll show you a better way for you to be: my way'. Sadly, this dynamic is too often believed to be the path to success in our world and workplaces, with traumatic consequences. I have been experiencing it in my leadership landscape, and I'm sure you too can find some examples for yourself, but as uncomfortable and saddening as it may feel, it is also an invitation for us to walk on the edge and change it.

It's easy to give our power away to others or try to exert power over them when we lack a strong inner foundation – our power within. **Standing in power within oneself** means having deep self-awareness and understanding of our purpose and our work in the world. It's living with value-based integrity and leading courageously as we walk on the edge.

To be able to stand in power with ourselves, we must first understand that true power originates from within; it is not something granted by others, but something each person uncovers and then cultivates for themselves. When we perceive power as external, we become subject to our environment – either surrendering responsibility and giving our power away or mistaking it for control and trying to dominate others.

When we are aware of our inner power, we have no need to be either submissive or dominant. Inner power isn't a scarce resource to be guarded. In fact, the more we tap into it, the more it expands. As it expands, it inspires and liberates others to tap into their own power within.

If we are ready to lead on the edge, there's one truth we must fully embrace: the only thing that will ever make us truly powerful is our power *within*. When we recognise power as an internal force, we gain mastery over ourselves and our responsibility to create change, regardless of external circumstances. The true transformation occurs when we unapologetically believe that we are enough to face any challenge as long as it makes the utmost sense to our identity and our purpose.

Without standing in power with ourselves, we will never feel truly powerful, because we will never feel truly free. Power and freedom are experienced by the bold – not by the faint-hearted or those hesitant to approach the edge. When we feel empowered from within, we walk on any edge with courage, consciousness and conviction.

Only when we're standing in power within ourselves can we have **power with others**, recognising that together, we can accomplish so much more than we can alone. The world is full of possibilities when we have power with others. It's about sharing power and joining forces for meaningful work.

Examples include large philanthropic initiatives such as that of UniCredit bank – one of my respected clients across many countries. UniCredit Foundation's new Edu-Fund Platform provides up to 14 million euros to support 'bold programmes that tackle educational deprivation in areas where UniCredit operates'.[74] By offering funding to non-profit organisations, the platform helps address issues affecting young people's education and enables underprivileged youth in Europe to develop their skills and knowledge.

Examples of having power with others can be found within smaller systems, such as teams where true collaboration and partnership replace the urge to be either the rescuing hero or the domineering boss. When power is shared, it empowers everyone and unlocks the full potential of each individual to contribute to meaningful change. Rather than wasting energy defending their importance or justifying their victimhood, everyone shifts their focus to genuine contributions beyond themselves.

Standing in power within ourselves, we don't only have power with others, we also **stand in power with the system** – the world we live in – recognising our responsibility to serve for the greater good and trusting in our innate boldness to be able to do that. Standing in power with the system is about our willingness to hear what the world needs, and then take action to serve those needs. It's about seeing the bigger picture and understanding our role within it, leveraging our influence for the greater good.

Even though there are not currently many examples of this, there are leaders who deeply understand that their primary responsibility is to serve, and this belief is reflected in their courageous business decisions. You can choose to call their approach idealistic, or you can choose to see it as their courage in redefining power dynamics to lead with a purpose that goes beyond the traditional metrics of business achievement.

Here's a great example. In September 2022, Yvon Chouinard, the billionaire owner of Patagonia, made an extraordinary move for environmental conservation when he chose to give away his company to aid the fight against the climate crisis.[75] This decision set a new benchmark for corporate leadership in environmental protection.

Patagonia's bold announcement was clear: 'From now on, Earth is our only shareholder. All profits, indefinitely, will be dedicated to our mission of "saving our planet".' In an act of commitment to this mission, the Chouinard family donated 2% of all shares and the control of decision making to a trust responsible for maintaining the company's values. The remaining 98% of Patagonia's shares were assigned to a non-profit organisation combating environmental crises with utmost urgency.

Chouinard's intention was to prevent the alteration of Patagonia's core values that might come with selling the company or going public. He stated, 'Instead of going public, we're choosing to go purpose.' In essence, rather than deriving value from nature for investor profit, Patagonia's generated wealth will be used to safeguard the very source of all wealth: nature itself. Through this bold decision, Patagonia communicated its relationship with power: power is there to serve.

How do all these forms of power come together? Moving beyond the dynamic of giving our power away or exerting it over others to a place where we feel centred in ourselves, unafraid to share power and united in power with the world represents a radical shift in how we perceive power. It's not about feeling too insignificant to effect change nor about trying to control everything; rather, it's about standing firm in our integrity and collaborating with others to achieve great good in the world. In this way, power evolves into a mature form of profound care. Allowing this evolution in itself means walking on the edge.

For power to become care, we must start by understanding the demands of our world. Recognising the needs of our world begins – again – with our power to question.

Power is everywhere. It exists in every relationship, and everything that exists is in some sort of relationship. Even when we are by ourselves, we are in a relationship with ourselves. Understanding power and daring to own and share it means having the ability to be bold in the way we relate to everyone and everything.

No meaningful change is possible without power. We need power to fuel our missions. To create the change we desire, we must first explore power to be able to reconnect with it, embracing it as a force of good that, when used skilfully, can change our world.

Conversations about power are uncomfortable, but they are essential – starting with the one you have with yourself. Where does your power lie? Understanding that is where your true leadership on the edge begins.

Intellectual boldness

When I was around seven years old, a peculiar habit came into my life: I would rearrange the furniture in my room on an almost monthly basis. The contents were few – just my bed, wardrobe, a couple of bookshelves and my desk – but these pieces would find themselves in countless configurations against the walls throughout the year. If a month passed without a shuffle, my mother would actually become concerned.

This ritual of rearrangement energised and motivated me. Take it as a great predictor of my love for change. Fast forward forty years and it seems like a valuable skill, don't you think?

Many people don't like change; too many leaders are among them. In his book *Ten Years to Midnight*, Blair H Sheppard shares how people respond to the fact of their changing world: 'I want the world to look like it did. I was more optimistic in the world I knew before.'[76] You get it – a key question is, what's your relationship with change? Do you continuously want the world to look like it did? Our relationship with change speaks about how willing we are to disrupt, learn and innovate – some of the key leadership tasks.

An insightful article from Korn Ferry titled 'Leadership is evolving. Are you?' goes so far as to ask if we have the so-called 'brain for change'.[77] That means leaders need to be 'voracious learners... By devouring new content and ideas, they'll stay ahead of rapidly shifting trends to make timely decisions on big issues.' In other words, we should be ready to spot emerging changes and constantly challenge both personal and system boundaries to discover better, bolder new solutions.

There are so many clients of mine who would love to hit the pause button on change. They ask, if something already goes well, why change? If it's not broken, why fix it? Here's the thing: the task of leadership is generally not to maintain the status quo, but to create a new future reality. It is to change the present into a better future. Essentially, the task of leadership is change.

Moreover, with our brains set for change, innovation is not strictly reserved for products and services, but it's for us as individuals too. We must self-innovate because we cannot really transform anything without transforming ourselves. That is quite a walk on the edge.

One of the aspects of our self-innovation that brings discomfort is this: being merely human, we never know if we are enough. That essentially means never knowing if we're already enough or good enough, or... you add to the list. Intellectual boldness is the courage to experiment with new knowledge, new ideas, new identities on the edge, and then adapt when necessary.

Being intellectually bold means finding the sweet spot where you are ready enough to walk the path along the edge before you cease to be relevant in your current reality, all while anticipating the next wave of change. It also means being bold enough to understand that if the path does not appear, we've got what it takes to create it by walking on the edge.

KEY IDEAS

- True leadership emerges when you leave the comfort of waiting at the edge and begin walking along the risky line, inspiring others to dream, learn and act.
- Leadership on the edge relies on three cornerstones:
  - **Vision**: a compelling image of a future worth risking for.
  - **Passion**: a grounding force that fuels persistence and inspires others.
  - **Grit**: the determination to persevere through setbacks, driven by activational hope and self-discipline.
- Leadership on the edge requires developing boldness in three dimensions:
  - **Emotional boldness**: normalising a full range of emotions as signals for growth.

- **Relational boldness**: navigating power dynamics with oneself, others and the system.
- **Intellectual boldness**: being in love with change, even amidst uncertainty.

Your mirror moment

Understanding ourselves is essential for taking action. Reflect on these key questions to sharpen your self-awareness:

1. What does walking on the edge truly mean to you?

2. For what change are you prepared to walk on the edge?

3. How can your vision, passion and grit not only bring others onboard, but also inspire them to walk on the edge with you?

Awareness without action is merely lost potential. Embrace true boldness by consistently confronting the emotional, relational and intellectual challenges of leadership:

1. **Emotions**. How open are you to the full spectrum of emotions in your leadership? Identify the emotions you must embrace to walk

on the edge. Like dipping your toe into water, start by exposing yourself to low-risk situations that will stir these emotions within you.

2. **Power**. Evaluate your relationship with power. Are you giving it away, exerting it over others or finding ways to share and stand in your power for the greater good? Reflect on your actions. What do you need to start doing differently? If you are unsure how, consider which beliefs about power you need to change to clarify the how.

3. **Change**. Identify areas where you resist change. What would it look like to accept just 2% of change? Start by implementing that small change.

SIX
Edge Walker Identities

Suzy Kassem, poet, philosopher and artist known for her writings on spirituality, politics and the interconnectedness of all things, believes that everybody possesses elements of both the sun and moon in them, balancing positive and negative energies that operate for them, against them and within them. To walk on the edge, we must calibrate these forces within us – our opposing identities.

Here's a glimpse into what I'm talking about, featuring short stories from three of my clients, shared with their permission. All three possess so many more qualities within them, but I'm sharing their stories through the lens of the identities that have had the most significant impact on how I perceive them.

Stoic and vulnerable (and so much more)
Managing director Asia-Pacific (APAC) (consulting, technology services and digital transformation)

On stage before the organisation's top 100 leaders, he spoke about an ambitious vision for the next five years, and then I witnessed him offering a startling truth: 'Firstly, I have no idea how we are going to achieve this; and secondly, I have no doubts that together, we will.'

The room seemed to hold its breath. From the front row, I thought, there are not many leaders I have seen who exhibit this kind of vulnerability openly on stage in front of their top 100 leaders. He did not blink. Instead, he smiled and proceeded to engage his audience, enrolling them into the future they would shape together, inviting them to sign up for the work and all the unknowns it would bring. Checking in with the people in the room, I could see they were fully on board.

Moments earlier, I had concluded my keynote on that same stage, incorporating an exercise that had the audience snapping their fingers in three distinct manners: initially to attune each individual to their own pace, then to synchronise with that of the person sitting next to them, and finally, to unite with the entire room's rhythm. This exercise, rooted in trust and connection, occasionally leads to everyone in the room snapping in harmony. You could argue that it just happens by accident or I help it happen by slowing people down, but my experience is that it *doesn't* always happen, regardless of me giving the same instructions in the same way every time. Some teams do not end up in sync, even after some time.

This team did. Somebody from the audience challenged the idea. Standing on the stage, my client invited everyone to start snapping, and they were immediately in sync. It was as if he was stoically showing a calm state of mind – the inner knowing, utmost trust and courage that it would work, after which he stepped just as courageously into his vulnerability in front of everyone. I could see that this leader trusted himself and his team, and that he was being trusted in return.

Six months thereafter, this leader was offered a new challenge: leading the organisation across the APAC region. This transition from his European home to completely unknown territories brought many complexities, including cultural ones, especially as he had to move his entire family. It was a reward for his successful track record and probably his craziness or boldness, depending on how you wish to name it, in embracing radical change in both his professional and private life.

He started this new role in September 2022, determined to shake things up. By November 2022, one of the first things he had done was organise the kick-off of a strategic initiative designed to empower the zone leaders.

This is the kind of leader who strikes you as being highly autonomous, yet his decisions regularly show-case his reliance on collective leadership. He knew that he'd be dependent on the community of leaders to move the organisation, unlock the potential and make a difference.

Many of his autonomous initiatives ignited radical changes. While he knew some of them would be more and some less welcome, he was aware that it would be the ownership and commitment of his team that would eventually sustain them all. Always strong in setting the direction, he never sails the ship alone.

Autonomous and dependent (and so much more)

Country head, Europe (pharma)

We settled in a coffee shop near her office on a hot July afternoon. She wanted to meet and plan for the keynote I was scheduled to deliver to 100 key people in her organisation in September.

'These people have been through a lot of changes and there are many more ahead. I'd like them to learn about the power of bouncing back and navigating change with a pinch of optimism. Transformation is inevitable,' she said.

By November, we were in my office, reviewing her Leadership Circle Profile® results. She was honouring first-hand the fact that transformation is inevitable. As we sat with her wonderful profile scores between us, I thought, I've got an effective leader in front of me; the devil must be in the details.

I asked, 'What's your relationship with conflict?' Her reaction was immediate and clear.

'No, I'm not going there. I had enough of that at a young age in my family. Thank you, let's move on.' Years of practice had honed my intuition on when to invite someone to cross the edge of their current identity. I gently persisted, suggesting we park the idea for now.

At our next meeting, she said, 'Hm, let's unpack that relationship with conflict, shall we?' marking the start of her journey to redefine her view of it. This exploration concluded with her acknowledging that while she may never enjoy conflict, she could allow herself to engage with it when necessary.

This realisation was crucial in helping her navigate the balance between autonomy and dependence. Moreover, it became a powerful tool in her toolbox, enabling her to hold her ground and have uncomfortable conversations to make the impact she wanted, without bringing unleashed drama to her team or exhausting herself with doubts and self-judgement.

That was so important given her next huge challenge: a major restructuring of her country's operations. With strict targets and clear expectations, it was a daunting task. She could have felt overwhelmed or tempted to either dominate or please, but she chose a different path. She questioned everything, cared deeply, learned continuously, trusted her team and showed decisiveness. I guess you could say that she walked on the edge with grace.

She experienced moments of surprise at her own polarities: 'Is this possible without getting into an emotional vortex? Am I losing touch with myself and others, being totally insensitive?' The truth was, she wasn't losing touch with anything. She was simply being autonomous, knowing who she was and what she stood for, and dependent, listening to her environment, sharing her power while maintaining her strategic focus.

'Possibility is everywhere you look for it,' was her new motto. Envisioning the completion of the restructuring, she wondered if leading the organisation would be a big enough purpose for her or if there was more. She knew that her walk on the edge right then was shaping whatever was to come next for both her and the organisation. 'What is the change that wants to happen here? What role do I play in its unfolding? Who will we become as an organisation? Who will I become?' were just some of the many questions she asked.

Ambitious and humble
(and so much more)

CEO and co-founder, USA (enterprise solutions)

'I'm passionate about business as a force for good, for social justice. My vision is responsible AI stewardship, but you see, my unfulfilled dream is to become a tech entrepreneur. I never really made it,' he confessed.

'What do you feel is the impact of that unfulfilled dream?' I asked, aware that he had already created what many would call a more than successful business.

'I want to get clear about whether my vision is a result of my passion or my drive; if there is a mission beyond the mere task,' he replied. 'If I'm unable to differentiate between the two, how could I ever create a legacy?'

Few accomplished businesspeople and leaders would be so humble about themselves. At the time of this conversation, he and I had been working together for eight months as part of an individual leadership coaching programme called Becoming Bold. Throughout our sessions, I couldn't help but think how our world needs more leaders like him – leaders who believe that change starts with them.

That's exactly the reason why the world today is on the edge. We keep convincing ourselves that change is some abstract concept detached from us. It's not. The need for constant change lies at the core of our identity and our ways of being. There is nothing we can transform through our leadership without first transforming ourselves, or at least doing so in parallel.

I can hear some of you saying you'd need to leave your organisation for that to happen, but I'm here to tell you that it is exactly in the middle of your organisation where self-transformation can and must happen. The conviction that we as leaders *are* the change is what made this leader both ambitious and humble in the dream he held for the future of his organisation.

We are the change. That sounds wonderful as an empowering slogan, but it's quite messy in practice. One of the best ways to test how well you calibrate between ambition and humility is to examine your perspective on transformation within your landscape: what and who needs to undergo it? If you don't include yourself in the answer, you might be stuck at one pole of this identity – ambition.

That's why for many leaders, the conviction that we are the change remains just an uplifting message, but not for this leader. During our time together, he was reflecting, learning, experimenting, realising, resetting, risking again and integrating – he was doing the work. In fact, his utmost power and magnificence were that he believed he *was* the work.

His story reminds me of a quote I read, attributed to Carl Jung, which invites us to become not just who we are, but all that we are, claiming that there is still more of us to be discovered, forgiven, and loved. That is the most ambitious and humble work you'll ever undertake. It is the walk on the edge, but unlike this inspiring and extraordinary leader, not many choose to do it.

What kind of person am I?

The Nike advertisement titled 'Winning Isn't for Everyone' begins provocatively: 'Am I a bad person?'[78] The ad continues by listing personal qualities usually seen as negative, such as being single-minded, deceptive and power-obsessed, along with having a lack of remorse and compassion, and a competitive desire to take from others without returning anything.

It concludes by questioning whether these traits truly make someone a bad person.

Created for the 2024 Olympic Games, it ignited a firestorm of controversy and opposing reactions. Does this advertisement reflect the culture we want to promote? Is it the lesson we wish to teach our children? Wait – isn't that our reality? We have to face it.

I've wrestled deeply with this ad, understanding that there is no straightforward answer. The message, much like our world, is a blend of darkness and light – a profound paradox. The Nike ad reflects the harsh realities of our ways of being. In response to Nike's question about whether this makes us bad people, I say it simply makes us incomplete and thereby human.

Our dark side resides within us, hungry for the light to achieve wholeness. Walking on the edge is not an expression of anger, despite moments of intense fury. It is not an expression of delusion, even though there are times when we must stand by what others consider completely irrational. It is not an expression of obsession, though sometimes it feels like being obsessed is the only thing that will get us out by getting us through.

Walking on the edge is a deliberate choice coming from our whole centred self, a conscious response for the sake of what we fundamentally care about.

Contrary to Nike's assertion that 'winning isn't for everyone', I argue that walking on the edge is an option available to all, though not everyone may choose to embrace it.

The urgency of now calls for our agency. As an example, places in the Olympics are limited – there may not be another Games for four years, but why would an athlete miss the pressing opportunity to act now to win their place? When we know our context and our ways of being, it is time to step into action. Bold leaders truly embody boldness only when they act.

Our being fundamentally influences our doing. This is why understanding who we are in our context is essential for effective action. That means all of who we are – our light and our dark, and our potential to calibrate in between these polarities.

This is exactly the kind of being necessary for our leadership today: to love the world – or our vision of it – so much we'd walk on the edge for it. To see what that kind of agency looks like from the perspective of translating intention into action, we need to move into a realm of doing, which is exactly what Part 3 is about.

KEY IDEAS

- Human identity is a dynamic interplay of light and dark forces; balancing these polarities is essential to walking on the edge.
- Edge walkers blend vulnerability with stoicism, autonomy with dependence and ambition with humility to lead authentically.
- Walking on the edge is a universal potential, unlocked by the courage to face and navigate discomfort and challenges, both internal and external.

Your mirror moment

Edge walkers are authentic leaders who face discomfort head-on, but being your authentic self is an ongoing journey of exploration, not a destination with easy or definitive answers. Reflect on these questions and commit to practising allowing your awareness to grow and deepen over time:

1. Who are you, really? Pinpoint the key qualities you must balance to walk on the edge and lead the change you envision.

2. Begin practising balancing these qualities and notice the emerging identities you embody as you walk on the edge.

Your activation zone

- List your top three game-changing ideas from Part 2.

- Where, how and when will you apply these ideas?

- What will happen if you don't take action?

PART 3
DARING ON THE EDGE

Katherine Anne Couric is a journalist who made a significant impact in 2006 by becoming the first woman to solo host a weekday evening news programme on a major US network with CBS Evening News. She is often attributed with stating that changing the world isn't about one big bang, but rather the accumulation of a billion tiny sparks, emphasising that some of those sparks will have to come from you.

As I've mentioned before, while many things don't make sense in this world, we still lack some good, bold, irrational ideas. More importantly, we lack the individuals eager to act on them.

I've repeated quite a few times that the world is on the edge. We feel different pressures in our leadership landscape today, to the point that they are our circle of constant uncertainty. At the same time, our landscape always remains our circle of impact – a context that has the power to inspire our sparks. If we then fail to bring those sparks into action, we'll fail to make a real difference. In fact, we'll fail to live a larger life away from mediocrity.

In our circle of impact, there's always a space where we can have real influence – the arena where we bring our sparks. Earlier, I explained that our arena is the specific space in our landscape where we choose to activate our sense of agency and bring bold leadership into action. In this space, our sense of agency, though sometimes deemed irrational by others, makes perfect sense to us, empowering us to take action on what truly matters, to do something about anything that's important to us.

It's crucial that we identify what that space is for us – that we claim our arena. By claiming it, we feel a compelling urge to act within it. It's where our care transforms into an active sense of ownership, where we begin walking on the edge – the edge of the change we seek to create.

Our walk on this edge becomes the very essence of our commitment to the change that we wish to see.

It involves walking away from a mindset of power-lessness, indifference or selfishness, and towards the mindset of decisive action. This is how it works: we shift from our inner monologue that's saying, 'There's nothing I can do about it' or 'I must do everything about it' or 'I don't want to do anything about it' to a resolute voice: 'I'm going to do something about that.' This transition empowers us to take bold steps, convincing us that everything changes when we do. Once we know that, we dare to act.

In Part 3, I'm going to show you examples of how that looks. I'll do that through real stories of real people who dared to act on what you may call an irrational idea. One of them, disturbed by the fact that some people are homeless and therefore excluded from society in many ways, came up with an idea to invite them to play football and travel around the globe, offering a framework for them to get their life back.

Another decided to swim unprotected in the ocean for more than two consecutive days to bring hope that everything is possible to anyone who is struggling to find a way out of their utmost fear, worry and discomfort. Then there are those who took no more than a second to decide to jump into dark, cold waters, swimming for their and other people's safety against all odds when, as refugees, no one wanted them, before one went on to swim in the Olympics where everyone celebrated them.

We will meet a man who made the shocking call to anaesthetise perfectly healthy children. They didn't need an operation, but this bold move still saved their lives. Finally, there is a woman who's dared to claim she's got a solution to eradicate poverty in no more than five years in a society where 14 million people, including 4.2 million children, struggle to make ends meet. Doesn't that all sound completely irrational to you? If it does not, then I must be far more mediocre than I'd ever like to think I am.

Irrational or not, one thing we need to agree on is that bold leaders are only bold in action, when they do their work. Part 3 is all about the doing. A leader on the edge is the one who dares to act. Simplicity has the power to move us into action, hence I've sorted the actions of leaders daring on the edge into four main realms. I have also captured the process of daring on the edge in four main stages. When I say process, this is what I mean: knowing your bold spark and your arena, starting your work, doing your work, completing your work, and then starting all over again. I'm speaking of daring to act on the edge while being on a quest. A leader without a quest is hardly a leader.

What actions does the leader on the edge take and what does daring on the edge look like when you're on your quest? That's what we're about to explore in the coming chapters.

SEVEN

In Action

If you're anywhere close to my age and hoping to live to about eighty or ninety years old, you've got around 2,000 weeks left. That's half of what Oliver Burkeman discusses in his book *Four Thousand Weeks*, where he puts our lifespan into painful perspective and brings urgency to our work.[79] I don't know about you, but I would have hoped we'd have many more weeks than that from the start.

ME→ (NOW WHAT?!)

MY LIFE

With this figure, you can choose to get demoralised or you can choose to get activated. If you choose the latter, I'd love to offer some clear actions that you can take.

The SOUL Framework®

My book *Bold Reinvented* centres around a leadership model called The SOUL Framework®.[80] SOUL stands for Self, Other, Universe and Legacy, and the framework is a roadmap for raising awareness of your bold leadership potential.

Here's a brief overview of each realm:

- In **Self**, you're discovering your identity that is big and bold enough for what you wish to do for the sake of your purpose.

- In **Other**, you're taking your leadership from transactional to relational, understanding that while it requires boldness to impact relationships with others, you cannot achieve anything important alone.

- In **Universe**, you're focusing on the systems in which you operate – your family, organisation, team and community – and learning about

the importance of your voice to initiate
bold conversations that bring change in
those systems.

• In **Legacy**, you're fully aware of the work that
you love and are committed to bringing it as a
bold leader in service of your world.

The SOUL Framework® reveals the boldness potential that's innate within you. It offers four realms
to awaken this potential – a strong foundation, but
there's more. To truly access your boldness beyond
merely deepening your awareness of it, you must
activate it through action, which is what Part 3 invites
you to do.

Therefore, each of these four realms is linked to a
critical action of walking on the edge. These actions
are by no means the only ones that can be taken
within their respective realms, but I see them as
being pivotal.

Let's dive in and discover how these four actions
integrate with The SOUL Framework® to guide you
in daring on the edge. In other words, let's activate
your SOUL.

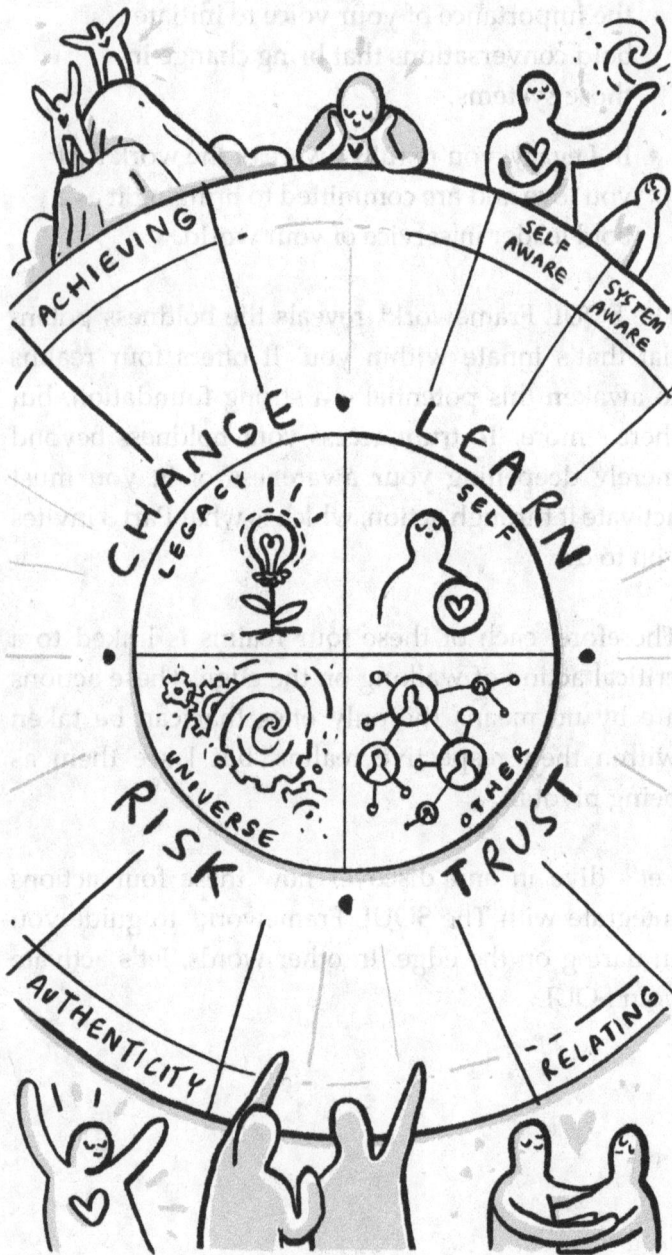

Self = learn

Self is all about revealing a bold and expansive identity that aligns with your purpose. As you **learn** about yourself and the world, you gain insight into the changes you aspire to make. You also identify your own patterns of thought and behaviour that either support or hinder your efforts for change.

Leadership begins with self-leadership, and that starts with an insatiable curiosity to learn about everything, including ourselves. This learning not only informs us, it also empowers us. We sometimes avoid learning at all costs because when we learn, we must act. To dare to act on the edge, we must first learn what within us puts us on that edge, and what in the world makes it worth the risk to walk there.

Other = trust

Other emphasises the power of deep, transformative connections in leadership. Recognising the boldness required at this level, it acknowledges that extraordinary achievements are not solo endeavours. Ideas can only fully flourish and continue to do so through trust-based relationships with others.

Trust, then, is a bold choice – a proactive commitment to give your best and call for the best in those around you. Once you decide to dare to act on the edge, choosing to trust is essential because it has the power to get you started. Trust that nothing and no one is there by chance – neither your ideas nor the people around you.

Universe = risk

Universe is about channelling your boldness through your voice to influence the broader systems in which you operate, initiating change irrespective of your formal position or authority. Often, it means swimming against the current and questioning norms. It's where your care transforms into an active sense of ownership, sometimes in a split second, resulting in contributions made not in spite of risks, but precisely because of them.

Being committed to daring on the edge means continuously seizing the opportunity to sit in the middle of the fire and embrace **risk**.

Legacy = change

Legacy centres on recognising and pursuing the love of your soul – a true expression of your deepest passions. It's about serving your world boldly with your most impactful work, the only path to creating lasting, meaningful **change**.

Daring on the edge, both literally and metaphorically, demands activating your SOUL. It calls for awakening your deepest self to find meaning in every risk and to embrace your innate boldness. Practically, it's a cycle: learn, trust, risk, change – and repeat.

While you may wonder how to apply this cycle to walk on the edge, the more urgent question should be *what for*? This question is about your *why* in action. While your why reveals deeply personal motivations, asking what for shifts focus beyond personal benefit. Once you understand what for – or for the sake of what – the *how* becomes clearer and more authentic, often requiring only one cycle of four pivotal actions as a reminder.

Leadership Circle Profile®

It will probably come as no surprise to you that I have linked these four pivotal actions to the creative dimensions of the LCP®. Here's how each action of your walk on the edge integrates with key LCP® dimensions:[81]

Learn – self-awareness and systems awareness

Learn will enable you to understand the difference that you want to make in a specific arena in your landscape and why, as well as how to get out of your own way so you can do that. In the LCP®, it's the action I'm connecting to the creative dimension of *self-awareness*, which reveals how active you are in growing your wisdom and knowledge. I'm also connecting it to the creative dimension of *systems awareness* because that informs you of the perspectives and orientations from which you lead as a start, taking into consideration the whole system and how you're in service to it as a leader.

Trust – relating

Trust will help you realise what it means to show up in your arena in front of others and how to see the potential to create radical connections with and allies from not just everyone, but also everything. In LCP® terms, this action is connected to the creative dimension of *relating*, measuring your capability to relate to others in such a way that brings out the best in everyone and – in our case – everything, including the idea itself.

Risk – authenticity

Risk will explore what it takes to continue walking on the edge and making bold decisions when it becomes messy in your landscape. In the LCP® lens, you risk when you stand firm in the creative dimension of *authenticity*, which reflects your courageous choices made in a high-integrity manner, even if they happen in a split second.

Change – achieving

Change as an action will clearly show what real change you have created or are creating as a result of your actions, and how it sets a foundation for others to build upon. In LCP® terms, this is connected to the creative dimension of *achieving*, a testament to the decisiveness needed to step up and act, even if in uncertainty, for a clear, purposeful vision.

While I will offer sufficient explanation for these connections to make sense to you, I encourage you to learn more about the LCP® outside of this book.[82] This will help you deepen your understanding of the perspectives behind the links I've made and will likely inspire you to consider measuring your own leadership effectiveness using this tool, especially if you are about to initiate and lead significant change. The LCP® provides valuable insights into how effective a leader you are and helps you lead on the edge to drive meaningful change in your arena.

We'll set off from what's always been a great starting point – let's learn.

Learn

Here's a game changer: deep learning expands your capacity to care. Care pulls you to act. Once you learn, you have to act. It really is that simple. The learning that I'm talking about is the one that deepens both your *self-awareness*, making you increasingly capable of honouring your own fundamental choices, and your *systems awareness*, improving your leadership landscape.

What do we learn about? We learn about the world and what's been normalised in it. We learn about ourselves and how we move through our world. This awareness empowers us to identify the aspects of both ourselves and our world we wish to transform.

The world

Firstly, let's speak about the world. In September 2022, world leaders gathered to inspire action on poverty, hunger, inequality and other global issues that translate into the seventeen United Nations (UN) Sustainable Development Goals (SDGs).[83] This is how Amanda Gorman, poet, activist and UN International Children's Emergency Fund (UNICEF) supporter, addressed them: 'I only ask that you care before it's too late, that you live aware and awake, that you lead with love in hours of hate.'[84] She made a great impact, ending with the touching invitation: 'Above all, I dare you to do good, so that the world might be great.'

To make our world great, there's some good work to be done by us leaders. That good work starts with us learning about what's important for us on the inside and what we wish to create in our outer world, coming from our inner sense of conscious care. However, sometimes holding the vision for our world may be paralysing.

Take, for example, the seventeen SDGs set as a vision for the world – a comprehensive blueprint for a better, more sustainable future for everyone. If you visit the UN's website, you'll see these goals presented as essential responses to huge global challenges, with a target for achievement by 2030. I'm not going to go into what gets in the way of transforming these ideals into concrete results on a collective global political level; instead, I'll speak about the power of the individual. One challenge lies in each of us seeing these goals as too big to connect to our own sense of agency, our own power to act.

Take Goal 1: no poverty. As individuals, we can find it too overwhelming to see how we can make any difference, and this is not just the case for the SDGs. It happens with many other goals for change set in front of us. We tend to overlook their potential to guide our individual actions within our leadership landscape, to crystallise the spark that could come from us.

As a result, we fail to see our own arena behind them. We miss the potential to get inspired to specify the difference we want to make, where we want to make it and what is important to us about making it. To be able to do that, we need to look at the big, overwhelming goal and get granular about it, or we risk taking no action where we could have changed the world with our more or less irrational idea.

Normalising the wrong things

Secondly, let's consider what's been normalised in our world, now we understand that changing the world has never been about changing *the* world. It's always been about the agency we bring to *our* arena within *our* landscape; about the actions we take in our circle of influence within our wider circle of impact.

That said, we must remember that our arenas vary; what feels like an arena to some may seem like the entire world to others. Somebody may choose to upgrade the mindsets of organisational leaders across the globe, somebody else to eradicate poverty in their own country, and another to focus on taking care of their community in whatever way possible. It's not about the size of the arena; it's what we tend to do as humans that prevents us from claiming our arena or taking any action in it.

In other words, we normalise the wrong thing. We tend to normalise the world's reality, and we numb – thus disempowering – our emotional response to it. Instead, we must normalise our emotional response to the current reality of the world as a starting point for empowering a different one – as a starting point for empowering change.

What's an example of this? We see homeless people on the street and normalise it while suppressing our emotion of pain because of it, instead of normalising our emotion of pain at the sight of people living without a home and allowing it to move us into doing something about it. Instead of normalising the emotion, we normalise the broken reality. This prevents us taking action where the emotion could tell us what the current reality is that we want to transform. It stops us from asking the single most empowering question that could kick off that transformation.

Let me tell you about that question. I remember taking the evening train from Woking to Havant in the UK, off for a few days of solitary writing of this book on Hayling Island. The carriage was completely empty and I chose a random seat. As I sat down, my eyes were drawn to a banner displayed in the train, a simple ad for a waste management company. It read: 'Change begins with what if…'

Some questions that may come to mind are:

- What if governments allocated military budgets to address social inequality and poverty instead?

- What if corporations placed environmental sustainability ahead of profit margins?

- What if societal norms valued emotional intelligence as much as academic achievement?

- What if technology companies prioritised user wellbeing over maximising screen time and engagement?

- What if communities prioritised mental health support and resources as much as physical health services?

What's the 'what if' that comes to *your* mind? Perhaps it's the one most relevant to your leadership landscape. How might initiating that what if conversation lead to the change that you'd want to create? If a part of you just thought, 'Yeah, right', that very fact highlights how our habit of normalising the wrong things can undermine our agency at its core.

You

Thirdly, let's go back to us – or, more precisely, to you. What is your personal leadership competitive advantage in your landscape and how do you know? Let me phrase that differently: if you did not exist as a leader in your landscape (your team, your organisation), what would be the solutions that others would miss and why? That's how I love to open conversations with senior leaders in organisations, pointing them towards their unique potential to take action so that we can then discuss how that agency potential gets blocked.

This blockage of our agency potential occurs in the machine called our mind. Our mind can be a possibility killer more often than we'd like to admit. Our actions, much like those of machines, are shaped by our complex internal structure: the operating system of our mind. Two fundamental mind structures shape our agency: the safe mind and the great mind.[85] Here's how that happens.

The moment you get anywhere close to the edge, your safe mind stops you there, begging you to wait, fuelled by anxiety about what's at risk. What your safe mind is actually doing is mitigating fear and easing internal discomfort by instilling a sense of safety. It does so instead of activating your agency for the change you seek to create, most probably because you don't know what that change is. Your focus is elsewhere.

With your safe mind, you only focus on whether there's fear. No fear, no impulse to react. Feeling safe lessens the motivation and the creativity to act. We could say that your safe mind puts your sense of agency to sleep, because it gets you away from the edge and therefore away from your true work.

Your great mind is built differently. It has the gritty capacity to acknowledge risks without letting fear dominate. In your great mind, vision leads with bold steps towards what truly matters. This mind redefines the usual, the ordinary, the rational, and normalises the uncomfortable. With each action that takes a step closer to the change you seek to create, your passion grows, fuelling even greater love for what you care about and what you're ready to risk for it.

Your great mind is a possibility creator. It's your companion on your walk on the edge. We all have a great mind, but it needs clear authority to override the programmed system within us that prioritises safety above all else.

Benjamin Zander, founder and music director of both the Boston Philharmonic and the Boston Philharmonic Youth Orchestras and co-author of *The Art of Possibility*, identifies three potential responses to life's challenges: anger, resignation or possibility.[86] I believe that only the latter is fuelled by love. The first two originate from fear, and while they may initially move us into action, they fail to sustain us and support the expansive potential for change that we can bring to our leadership landscape by walking on the edge. Fear cannot last as indefinitely as love can.

Just as love endures indefinitely, the human soul is free and can never be tamed, yet we spend our entire lives attempting to do just that. Learning sets our souls free because it brings to our awareness a wide range of limiting beliefs that we blindly follow until we learn otherwise.

Think of your limiting beliefs as the mental barriers you create that hold you back from reaching your full potential and living a joy-full and soul-full life. These are deeply ingrained stories you tell yourself, often unconsciously, convincing yourself that you're incapable of achieving what you deeply desire or, even worse, that you're unworthy of success. Limiting beliefs act like invisible chains, keeping you stuck in familiar patterns of mediocrity and preventing you from exploring new possibilities of extraordinariness.

I have previously explored three narratives we tell ourselves when we retreat into safety and remain waiting at the edge: I can't do anything about it, I must do everything about it and I don't want to do anything about it. Additionally, I've identified sixteen other stories in the form of personal limiting beliefs that I frequently hear in my conversations with leaders. While I've grouped these sixteen stories around four fatal fears: failure, being wrong, rejection and emotional discomfort, a concept developed by psychologist Maxie Maultsby who believed these fears can significantly block us,[87] each belief is multifaceted, often merging different fears.

I invite you to identify which beliefs might be hidden in your own safe mind. This exploration is not about finding the right answers; it's about raising awareness that can unlock your bold actions once you've shed light on what may be limiting you, keeping you trapped in moments – or years – of inaction.

Fear of failure narratives

- **Risking is irrational**. 'The higher up you go, the less you want to risk. My role, status and reputation mean a lot to me. I've earned them through hard work. Now, with so much at stake, risking it all just doesn't make sense. It would be totally irrational.'

- **I'll be laughed at for dreaming big**. 'Why try something no one has done before? Why would I ever think I could be greater than the majority of others? Whoever thinks they can is bound to be ridiculed eventually.'

- **No big deal**. 'I don't see my ideas as a big deal. Playing small keeps me improving and realistic about my limits, which is key for solid success.'

- **Stay driven**. 'Pausing to reflect on my purpose may lead to a downfall. There's no time for that, and even if I did uncover it, my environment wouldn't allow me to act on it. I'd just fall behind. Staying driven is the only way to keep up.'

- **Change is a myth**. 'Staying on top means not rocking the boat. That's how it's always been. Success is a game of trade-offs. Changing that is a myth.'

Fear of rejection narratives

- **No upsetting**. 'True leaders navigate without upsetting others, staying away from conflicts and leading without clashes. They avoid irrational initiatives that could create disagreements.'

- **Extraordinary isolation**. 'Trying to do something extraordinary is a double-edged sword. It can push people away because they no longer see you as one of them.'

- **Harmony over initiative**. 'Taking my initiative puts pressure on me to meet others' expectations, risking disappointment when I choose their needs over mine. Staying passive feels safer and smarter for keeping harmony and my own sense of calm.'

- **Conform or clash**. 'Breaking the rules makes you a target for criticism or rejection. If everyone challenged the norms, chaos would follow.'

- **Safe humility**. 'Stepping back is smart and safe. Leading might seem bossy and push people away. Besides, others know more than me about this. Valuing true expertise has always been key for me.'

Fear of being wrong narratives

- **No vulnerability**. 'People shy away from harsh truths everywhere. Being totally honest isn't always welcome, even if everyone says it is. Vulnerability can make you seem less reliable, like everything else is false.'

- **Help is a risky business**. 'Asking for help feels like showing weakness and could make me look incompetent as a leader. It might lead to others taking advantage.'

- **Ready over relevant**. 'Boldness is not enough; you need to be prepared. It's not about the lack of courage; moving forward requires having the right information. Without it, you risk being an amateur.'

- **Expertise perfection**. 'My expertise demands perfection; any error is unacceptable. A mistake would damage my reputation for reliability, I'm certain of it.'

Fear of being emotionally uncomfortable narratives

- **Great idea, wrong time**. 'It's a good idea – but it would've been great years ago or years from now. Right now, it's just not the time (yet).'

- **Escaping the spotlight**. 'I've never liked being in the spotlight; it just doesn't feel right. Self-promotion isn't my style, especially when what I do isn't unique.'

What other limiting beliefs would you like to see on the list? Reflect on the above once more and feel free to add your own.

Whatever they are, limiting beliefs can make it easy for you to talk yourself out of what your great mind considers it worthwhile to achieve, so revisit them as many times as necessary. They exist beyond your immediate awareness, playing a role in taming your boldness for the sake of safety, security and comfort, and you might be reluctant to face them. It may take time to confront them fully, but this journey of learning has an inevitable outcome. Each time you step into your fear, the fear dissipates and you find yourself capable of making a meaningful difference, knowing exactly where and why.

Limiting beliefs persistently trap our daring soul in a confining box it was never meant to occupy. The change we deeply care about is too big and too bold for this box of protecting mental structures, but once we uncover our limiting beliefs, we realise our true potential to act cannot be boxed in.

There are failed systems everywhere. Our broken reality exists largely because we started and kept normalising it. One of the key learnings to awaken our sense of agency is to question if we're normalising the right thing, and if we're doing it from within or outside of the box, even if we are afraid of the answers. Of course, there's a paradox here – it's never that simple and it always is.

Trust

Elizabeth Gilbert, an American journalist and author best known for her 2007 memoir *Eat Pray Love*,[88] offers a fascinating perspective on ideas, suggesting they inhabit our world much like living beings, existing with consciousness and purpose, motivated solely by the desire to be realised. To accomplish this, ideas seek people to work with.

Gilbert says, 'The only way an idea can be made manifest in our world is through collaboration with a human partner.'[89] According to Gilbert, while we often overlook or dismiss ideas, those we choose to engage with seem to ask, 'Do you want to work with me?'

Following Gilbert's wisdom, do you believe that the change you care about could choose you? Even if it shows up in the form of an irrational idea, will you accept that it may pick you out from the mass of other leaders?

However strange, I invite you to trust Gilbert's bold perspective and start nurturing the relationship with your own idea that might have chosen you as its partner. That trust changes everything and expands your ways of *relating*. More precisely, it defines how you relate to your work, to others and even to yourself:

- How you relate with your arena and the change you seek to create (trusting your work).

- How you enrol others while walking on the edge (trusting others).

- How you give yourself permission while taking action (trusting yourself).

Trusting that your idea, your arena, your walk on the edge might have chosen you prompts you to start showing your most caring connection to them as if they are dear friends that you don't wish to keep waiting for your company.

When writing my first book, especially at the beginning, I felt moments of heaviness. I wanted it to be over; at times, I was literally disturbed by spending any time writing it. I loved the idea of my own book and wanted it to be completed; to stand as a testament to something I had created, but it was as though I was almost wanting to skip the process of creation itself and find myself immediately at the finish line.

A conversation with a leadership mentor changed my entire perspective. She asked: 'What do you love about spending time with your book? What's your way of communicating with it? Visualise your book as if it were your dear friend. How would you want to be with it every day? What is it that others might see when they watch you appreciate that relationship dearly?'

The thing is, these are questions you can apply to whatever your walk on the edge may be – especially when it feels most uncomfortable. Do you want it to end because of the discomfort or are you willing to engage with it, nurture your partnership, and trust – deeply, undeniably trust – that this partnership is there for a reason? What if that walk on the edge means thirteen years of court battles against the largest organisation in the country, or anything else from your landscape that gives you shivers? It's a radical perspective, or is it simply a bold one?

If you truly listen to her questions, you'll hear that my mentor wasn't just trying to get me to love my work, but to appreciate it in such a way that it would become an inspiration for both myself and others. Relating to the change you want to create is so important because it holds great potential to attract others. Hear this again: the way you relate to the change you wish to create will define who – if anyone – will join and support you. Think about that because you'll need allies in your arena.

Creating change is never a solitary sport. Walking on the edge and bringing agency to your arena is never about you being in the spotlight. Rather, it's about you *being* the spotlight. Let yourself radiate. I assure you, you will attract others. The more you radiate, the more allies you'll attract. The more allies, the greater the possibility for change.

Extend your invitation to others to join you in your work – it's called enrolment. People don't just enrol at a university or for another training course. They enrol into our ideas and initiatives every second, even into those considered irrational at first sight. Today, probably more than ever with such technological advancements, we are bombarded by all sorts of ideas faster than we can breathe. True enrolment is not just an invitation; it's an opportunity for someone to eagerly commit to joining you.

Enrolment begins with building trust and relationships, and it's beautiful if it ends with mobilising others around your vision of change. Here are some of the questions you may wish to ask potential allies:

- What do you like about the change that
  I care about?

- What does this change make possible?

- What could happen if this possibility is brought
  to life?

- What would make you passionate about
  joining me?

- How would you like to join me?

When you're inviting others to enrol into your idea, be clear about what you need from them for the sake of the change that you seek to create. Clarity will engender trust. In fact, clarity will increase trust over time, and then trust will keep increasing clarity in return. Be clear about what you do need, what you don't and what you don't know if you do. Be clear when you need help, and you will.

Trust can mean knowing you can do it alone but you don't have to just because you have the capacity to. Trust means knowing that there are things you cannot do alone, and that there are always solutions to that.

In the story of my world on the edge told earlier in the book, I've invited certain people to support me in my arena – I've seen them as allies. While some have joined in, others have acknowledged me for my persistence, even my courage, saying that they don't feel they can or want to join in. My arena, in which I'm taking a stand for my integrity against a large system, is just not their arena.

You'll never manage to enrol everyone. Let go of those that you don't. Those who need to will show up shoulder to shoulder with you. Let the others go. Trust that everything happens at the right time and for the right reason. Your arena is always somebody else's arena as well, but it's not everyone's arena, and neither should it be.

Give yourself honest and courageous permission for that to be so. Trust that you're worthy whether others approve of your arena or not, even those closest to you. It's your walk on the edge, not theirs, until they see their vision of change as part of the one you've brought to the table. Give yourself permission to be your own hero who trusts in one's own choice to walk on the edge, and whatever the outcome along the way, appreciate everything and everyone as your mentors. In the end, being mentored is always a choice. It's dictated more by your orientation to learn than by others' intentions to teach you.

Risk

Risk is about rising to meet the opportunities that present themselves. When you risk, you stand firm in your integrity and your courage; you lean fully into your *authenticity*. In fact, you lean into all of your authentic self. The messier things get, the more strongly you lean.

As you do so, here's what you are clearly communicating: 'Change starts with me; I must be the change I want to see in the world.'[90] This is what you are continuously asking yourself: 'As a leader on the edge, what opportunities are presenting themselves to me? How am I rising to meet them in an instant?'

Taking risks might not be easy, but it's fundamentally simple. You act on the need, the request that you perceive as an opportunity emerging in the moment. This is different from your unconscious drive to jump on any issue and ease the sense of discomfort. Rather, I'm talking about the situations that clearly call for a leader in front: someone to take a stand and take a risk now.

In these moments, you cannot explain or understand risk by rationalising it. It's a signal appearing and meeting your sense of knowing that it's yours to rise to. It speaks to your integrity and calls forth your courage. You take the lead – and the risk that comes with it – in any given moment. This isn't about a single risk; it's about making risk your mode of operation.

Understand that mode of operation as a decision that is aligned between your head, heart and gut in an instant: in other words, it is your full presence's readiness to take risks in any moment. Even though I'm not overly fond of tools, there is one I particularly like when I train new coaches, and it's based on the Transformational Presence approach by Alan Seale.[91] Seale is an author, speaker and coach who has developed this unique approach, which is designed to help individuals and leaders show up fully in their lives and work, creating positive change and inspiring others to do the same.

Transformational Presence emphasises the importance of being present, engaging both the intuitive and rational minds, and navigating complex situations with grit and action. Applying this approach helps people to connect with their authentic selves and the potential within their circumstances. The specific tool I'm using is about having a conversation between your head, heart and gut, which is needed to make a centred decision. You'd use it in cases when you're struggling to decide whether to act on something or not because for you, it represents a certain risk.

The conversation might go through questions like this:

- Who wants to speak first about this idea – my head, heart or gut? What does it say?

- Who wants to answer and with what message?

- Who's remained silent?

- Who's speaking all the time?

- Who seems to be arguing? Who might have a solution to that conflict?

- Who's worried and why?

- Who's afraid to speak?

- Who wants to be right and why?

- Who has given up?

- What do they all agree on? What not? How do I want to be with that?

You get the point. My experience is, the more frequently you have this conversation, the quicker you'll become at accessing the head-heart-gut alignment and wisdom. Practice is essential because you'll encounter many moments that present opportunities to rise. Contrary to the instincts of your safe mind, you won't have the luxury of time for lengthy internal debates to rationalise whether to seize them. To rise to these emerging opportunities, you'll need to make an intuitive decision to take the risk. In that moment. Right then. Instantly.

Often, taking a risk will feel like a fleeting opportunity – a cubic centimetre of chance appearing before you that you don't want to let slip by. The term 'cubic centimetre of chance' comes from anthropologist and writer Carlos Castaneda in the context of being more aware and perceptive.[92] It is a brief, unexpected opportunity that pops up in life. Every situation has one of these moments that you need to grab without delay. It's about the importance of full presence – paying close attention to everything around you so that you're ready to take hold of these small but important opportunities when they appear.

Life constantly offers cubic centimetres of chance, but they're easy to miss if you're not fully present or ready to act. They appear for all of us at various moments; the distinction between an ordinary person and a bold leader lies precisely in awareness. The true difference lies in the bold leader being 'alert, deliberately waiting, so that when his [sic] cubic centimetre pops out, he [sic] has the necessary speed, the prowess, to pick it up.'[93]

You won't ever spot your cubic centimetre of chance while waiting at the edge, focusing on safety. Your safe mind is incapable of recognising the momentum, your momentum, which is what the cubic centimetre of chance really is. It will miss it even if your momentum is strikingly obvious.

Your alertness, speed and prowess originate from your daring great mind – a fire deeply seated in your heart, a truth felt in your belly, a passion continuously present and alive. Whatever the outcome, you stay fully committed to the change you wish to create, which keeps you on your toes every single moment of your walk on the edge.

Essentially, taking risks is like surfing. You can't really grasp the experience by standing on the sand talking about it. You've got to grab your board, paddle out and catch the wave.

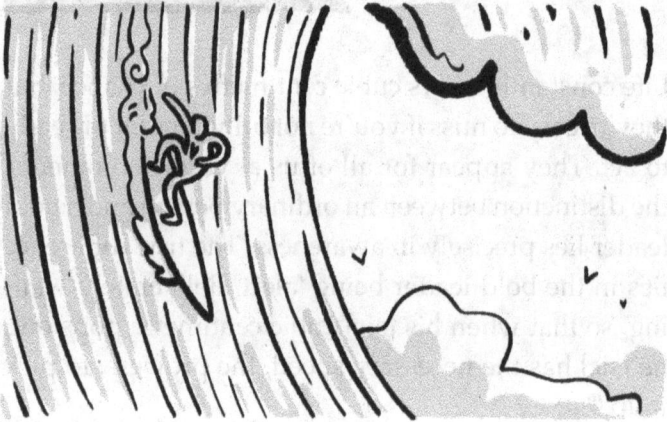

Change

Knowing what matters to you and the changes you want to see, you don't wait for others to lead the way, even though you include them. You move ahead, not held back by doubts, fears or conventional boundaries.

You're ready to act in a split second and face the risk. That, all together, is what eventually creates change.

Change will result in the new future coming from the present reality that you have achieved as an outcome of your actions. You'll leave it for others to build upon. In the Leadership Circle Profile®, the action of change reflects the creative dimension of *achieving*. The future is not something we enter; it's something we consciously design and purposefully achieve.

As Franklin D Roosevelt said, 'The only limit to our realisation of tomorrow will be our doubts of today.'[94] This reminds me of a film I enjoyed watching – *Father Stu*.[95] It's a true story about Father Stuart Long – a man who, after a failed boxing career and a near-fatal motorcycle crash, found his calling in the Catholic priesthood, even as he faced a shocking diagnosis of a fatal disease. There are two simple yet profound sentences from the film that have stayed with me: 'Our world is teaching us that there is comfort in knowledge and fear in the unknown. What if the unknown is greater than we could possibly imagine?'

Having seen the film, I can't help but wonder if Father Stu was actually able to imagine a glimpse of his great future beyond the doubts of his unknown journey. Initially, he thought he was just seeking a successful career, but when he realised that he wanted to become a priest, he discovered a commitment greater than the doubt-filled messages his family and even the Church were trying to tell him. Could he ever have truly imagined the profound impact he would have? His contributions significantly influenced systems, from small family dynamics to large institutional structures like the Church.

Once you expand your views beyond what is seemingly possible, you build up huge levels of inspiration for yourself and others. However, that is still not enough for real change to take place. In his seminal work *Servant Leadership*, Robert K Greenleaf speaks about everything beginning with the initiative of an individual: 'The very essence of leadership, going out ahead to show the way, derives from more than usual openness to inspiration.'[96] He also clearly underlines that the leader must do more than just inspire. As a leader on the edge, you need to act: to set direction, get going and keep going. Then coming full circle, you need to complete as well.

When we're creating change, completing is important. By setting a direction, unworried about what may seem possible and what seems almost irrational, we confirm that we believe we cannot fail in making a positive difference.

Another important element is to recognise when we have achieved what we intended – when the walk on the edge in effect ends. That's when we need to complete our work and celebrate the change – the act of actually embracing the change we have created. The thing is, embracing change can bring uncomfortable feelings such as fear of vulnerability and imperfection.

We can double check with ourselves if it's time to move on and where to by asking:

- What does my boldest look like? Have I given it?

- Does the new reality honour my fundamental choice? Have I created the change I envisioned?

- What do I dream of next? What's the work already calling me?

We know that the change has happened once we sense our inner readiness to start walking on a new edge. As with knowing when to begin and what direction to take, only we '…have the authority to recognize and confirm a result as complete,' Robert Fritz states, adding that: 'In the stage of completion, your being is ready for another act of creation.'[97] Equally important, your completed act of creation is ready for others to build on it with the change that they deeply care about, consciously or unconsciously finding inspiration in what you have left behind. That's how we build on each other's legacy.

Learn, trust, risk and change are the actions we take as leaders daring on the edge, determined to do something about what matters to us. Our walk on the edge looks like a combination of all these actions rather than their sequential occurrence one by one. If you look around in your leadership landscape, or perhaps look in the mirror, I'm sure you'll be able to identify different leaders on the edge with stories that reflect these actions.

I've collected a few such stories that have deeply inspired me. Each one has evoked in me a sensation, a feeling that the change is indeed more than possible, no matter how irrational it seems at the beginning. It's already there because these leaders are there, daring on the edge and ready to continue their walk.

I've grouped their walks on the edge into stages, aligning these stages with the actions we've just explored in an attempt to simplify the complexity. The reality and realness of each of these stories are, however, richer than that.

You can read them in the next chapter.

KEY IDEAS

- With a limited lifespan, you face a choice: be demoralised or activate your potential to create meaningful impact.
- Know The Soul Framework® and the critical actions of daring on the edge:
  - **Self**: discover a bold identity aligned with purpose.
    - o **Learn**: expand self-awareness and system-awareness to empower action and transformation.

- **Other**: build relational leadership to achieve transformative collaboration.
  - o **Trust**: develop deep, authentic connections with people and ideas, fostering collaborative boldness.
- **Universe**: influence systems with bold actions, taking ownership despite risks.
  - o **Risk**: stand in authenticity, making courageous decisions that push boundaries and create change.
- **Legacy**: commit to meaningful work that creates lasting change.
  - o **Change**: drive purposeful actions to achieve a vision and leave a foundation for others to build upon.
- Engage in a continuous loop of **learning, trusting, risking** and **changing**, guided by a clear sense of purpose (for the sake of what).

Your mirror moment

Wake yourself up with these questions:

1. Are you making the most of your limited time?

2. How?

3. What's in it for the world?

Then, activate your bold soul through four pivotal actions, allowing some time in between each one:

1. **Learn:** What do you need to learn about yourself and your leadership landscape to spark the change you envision? Deepen your insights about your *self-awareness* and *system-awareness* through LCP® assessment.

2. **Trust:** What idea has been quietly calling you, as if it's chosen you? What do you need to embrace to trust this idea fully? Share your idea with someone to start *relating* to it and bring it to life.

3. **Risk:** List the risks your idea might bring. Which one are you prepared to take on now? Are you playing it small or are you ready to bring your full *authenticity*? As you bring your idea to life, practise tuning into your cubic centimetre of chance using head-heart-gut awareness.

4. **Change:** Imagine the impact if your idea succeeds. What makes it extraordinary? Where are you letting mediocrity hold you back? What bold move could you make today to lead on the edge and *achieve* extraordinary change?

EIGHT

On The Quest

Now it's time to share a handful of stories that have profoundly inspired me. They've confirmed my belief that extraordinary change is not only possible, it's always in motion, thanks to leaders who are out there, daring on the edge. I have captured their journey from an irrational idea to the actual bold change they effected.

My aim is to provide a simple roadmap of the stages you will go through when daring on your own edge. I've called this process 'On the Quest' because when we walk on the edge, daring to act, we are in pursuit of something valuable (like discovering our bold self) and achieving something extraordinary (like creating a better world). You could say we're advocating for bolder leadership towards a better world.

4. COMPLETE & CELEBRATE

3. GET REAL & BOLD

2. GET STARTED & CONNECT

1. GET CLEAR & READY

For simplicity, to make engagement easier and prompt action, I envision our journey in four stages while we're on this quest, each linked to an action we discussed in the previous chapter:

- **Get clear and ready** (beginning with the **learning** process).
- **Get started and connect** (**trusting** your own idea).
- **Get real and bold** (taking a **risk** in a split second, making the decision that makes all the difference).
- **Complete and celebrate** (celebrating the **change** achieved and moving forward to create new ones).

As I will illustrate with several upcoming stories, leaders on the edge who dared to act on their bold ideas navigated these stages, moving away from mediocrity. They are real stories of real people with real impact. While all four stages – and thus all four actions – are inherently part of every adventure, each story inspired me profoundly at one particular stage, which I use as the focal point for presenting each leader's journey on the edge.

While I have personally interviewed some of these leaders and others not, all these stories are significant and deserve to be told. Depending on what the landscape in which you lead is, I am conscious that they might seem overwhelming and too detached from your reality. I invite you to consider two things.

Firstly, look at these stories as metaphors, drawing from their wisdom for your personal growth and your bold agency. Secondly, while you may consider them from a metaphorical perspective, remember that these are authentic tales of real people. They aren't mythical heroes or heroines from a distant past or unreal future, but individuals like you and me who have identified their arenas within their own leadership landscapes to make a difference. Crucially, they did not abandon their idea of effecting the change they so care about simply because it seemed too bold or irrational at the very start.

Get clear and ready

'I just don't believe that there should be any homelessness in the world. I don't know how we have allowed a system to emerge where a rich, economically powerful country has thousands of people on the street. There's something wrong. To me, it's completely unnecessary. We should not be living in a world like that. We should quite easily be able to create systems that stop that from happening.'

He spoke so clearly about his sense of agency. This is how it sounds when somebody refuses to normalise the reality that stands against their fundamental choice. It's not the way it should be and he was ready to do something about it.

He is Mel Young, a renowned social entrepreneur recognised for his significant contributions to addressing homelessness and promoting social inclusion. One of Mel's most impactful ventures, co-founded in 2001 with Austrian Harald Schmied, is the Homeless World Cup – an initiative that uses football to inspire and empower homeless people.[98]

I learned about Mel's story while watching the Netflix film called *The Beautiful Game*.[99] I was so inspired by that bold initiative that, realising it is based on a real story, I decided to look for Mel to have a conversation with him. I reached out to him on LinkedIn, and a few days later, I received a warm response. He agreed to meet me, share more about the change he believes in and explain how he's decided to make a difference.

'I came up with this idea of the Homeless World Cup in 2001 when I was having a beer with a colleague of mine called Harald Schmied.' From the moment he opens the story, I realise again and again how the people making some of the biggest changes can sound so ordinary, even though they are extraordinary in so many aspects. My fascination keeps growing as Mel continues his story.

'Both of us had our backgrounds in journalism and we were running street papers, which are produced for homeless people to sell. They keep the majority of the cover price for all the papers they sell. I was working in one in Scotland and Harald was working in one in Graz, Austria.'

He goes on, explaining to me how the organisation of street papers was fragmented worldwide, prompting Mel and Harald to create an association to bring these efforts together. Despite limited funds, they managed to convene annually, creating a sense of community and mutual support. These conferences, Mel says, were 'consistently upbeat and inspiring', providing an adrenaline boost for participants to sustain their sometimes challenging work with homeless individuals over the following year.

At the end of one such conference in Cape Town in 2001, Mel and Harald were having a beer and chatting. 'This is a great conference, but there are no homeless people here. We're being inspired, but we're either editors or founders or whatever. How could the homeless people experience what we're experiencing?'

Mark this moment. The instant we realise that there is something important to be created, our safe mind kicks in, telling us why it's impossible – who would get visas and passports for the homeless? What language would the conference use? None of it would work.

Then the first what if moment occurred for Mel and Harald. 'There's an international language called football.' Again, some smallness sneaked in to suggest creating one team in Scotland and one in Austria and bring only these two together to play.

I notice the spark in Mel's eyes as he continues to tell me about the moment his great mind stepped in again: 'We said, look, why don't every country come? You know, why not? Why just us two? And let's call it the Homeless World Cup, and so we agreed we'd do that.'

The next morning, Mel and Harald met at breakfast, reflecting on their conversation. 'Would we leave it in the bar – because you can do that sometimes – or would we do it? This was actually the important moment. Yeah, we said, let's do it.' They both took on their separate roles and started to work, being clear about the change they sought to create and their own eagerness to activate their agency.

That marked the beginning of what we know today as the Homeless World Cup, a football tournament with a purpose, as Mel and Harald described it themselves. Their website states: 'Our year-round work culminates in a world-class event which has the power to transform the lives of participants and shape attitudes towards homelessness.' After the first Homeless World Cup in Graz, Austria, in July 2003, seventeen more tournaments followed across the world, one each year except for during the pandemic. The tournament has brought together participants from around the globe, with events held in various continents including Europe, Africa, the Americas and Australasia, hosted in diverse locations – from the bustling cities of Gothenburg and Edinburgh to the vibrant atmospheres of Cape Town, Melbourne and Mexico City to the carnival vibe of Rio's Copacabana Beach.

As I write this book, the 2024 event took place in September at Hanyang University in Seoul, making it the first-ever Homeless World Cup hosted in Asia, and it was a fabulous success. What started as an exchange of almost irrational ideas in a conversation between two bold people committed to doing something about what they refused to normalise has turned into a movement. It's turned into a change that today – more than twenty years later – keeps impacting millions of lives.

The first Homeless World Cup involved sixteen countries, the teams based around the different street papers. Mel and Harald made the rules, stipulating the size of the pitches, that each team would sing their country's national anthem and play in the city selected to host. In other words, they created a real football competition. However, some of their attempts to enrol others were discouraging at first, as Mel recalls.

'I would say, "Why don't you sponsor this?" and they would reply, "What are you talking about?"' The final outcomes rewarded their actions of trust, though. 'Between the pair of us, we managed to make it happen, although we didn't really know what was going to happen. We had ideas and we were optimistic about what we thought the outcomes would be, but they were much greater than anything we ever could have imagined.'

Ahead of the 2024 event, for the first time, FIFA agreed to support the Homeless World Cup Foundation by broadcasting the tournament across various platforms and providing materials and equipment, including medals and trophies.

'People flocked to watch the Cup, filling the venues every day, and the players' reactions were incredible,' recalls Mel about the early days of the event, which shifted the perception of homeless individuals away from stereotypes. He highlights the impressive outcomes from a player survey conducted during the Homeless World Cup in Cardiff in 2019: 94% of the participants reported that the event had a positive impact on their lives, 83% noted improved social relations with family and friends, 77% stated that the experience significantly changed their lives and 76% continued to enjoy and play the sport. Mel proudly shares these statistics, underscoring the transformative power of the event.[100]

The players are the most important part of the Homeless World Cup, but the spectators are also crucial, cheering and transforming their view of the players. Instead of ignoring or shunning them, people now ask for their autographs and take selfies with them. In Mexico City, 167,000 people came to watch over eight days. The global media have covered the event positively, unlike their usual negative portrayals of homeless people.

The success of the first event inspired Mel and Harald to continue and the Homeless World Cup has grown each year, impacting over a million lives. The Homeless World Cup Foundation is now in seventy countries, influencing governments and systems to address homelessness, believing that no one should be without a home.

Mel also speaks about the times when the Homeless World Cup faced a resource crisis and had to cancel events for several years due to the Covid pandemic, nearly deciding to stop altogether. Despite the difficulties, the seventy initiatives worldwide have continued their work and managed to get back on track with, as he calls it, 'brutal determination'.

To my comment that everything depends at a certain point on one person who's willing to take a lead, take a stand, take a risk, he gives himself permission to reply: 'Well, that was me. I couldn't imagine stopping. I mean, we had to get it on. Cities now, they're all over us, but at that point, nobody wanted to host it. It just wasn't easy, but we pulled it off. We did it because I knew and understood what the benefit was, and by not continuing, we would be letting people down.'

When I ask him what has kept that fire burning inside of him, he's clear about the role of others who stand shoulder to shoulder with him. 'It's not just me, by the way; there's a fantastic team of people in our own organisation, but also in the seventy countries. Maybe I'm the leader, but nothing works unless there's followers, if you like; unless there's other people there. These people are brilliant and they're leaders in themselves.'

Recalling some of the work they've done together that has been incredibly difficult, Mel speaks about what keeps him going. 'I'm absolutely sure it is the outcomes. We're obviously a charity, so we don't make money, but I speak to the homeless people who are players, and they tell me their stories about how they've changed. I spoke to someone just the other day from Sweden. She had become an alcoholic, but through the football, she managed to get sober, and she is now at university studying law. She is aiming to do a master's in criminology. I'm looking at her and she's talking away to me about her life and what's happened and the football and everything, and that's my profit. I get hundreds of these moments of profit. I know that what we're doing is actually making a real difference to people's lives. That is what keeps me going.'

This is what Mel dreams of from here: 'How do we create a situation where people stop playing [in the Homeless World Cup] because they're not homeless?'

First, he highlights the systemic failure and the need for solutions rather than just discussing the problem. To address this, he and his allies have started gathering different solutions and compiling them into reports, which are shared at their annual events.

Then, he shares a story to illustrate one of their solutions. At the first event in Austria, the Austrian Football Association lent the Homeless World Cup referees. One referee enjoyed the experience so much that he wanted to return, and over the years, many referees from around the world have been volunteering their time. This has led to one of them creating a programme to train homeless individuals to become referees, providing them with employment opportunities and a path to professional refereeing. What a wonderful example of someone building their good work upon someone else's great legacy.

'Sometimes, when I'm trying to explain how the Homeless World Cup works to older people, they kind of look at me a bit blankly. When I explain it to schoolchildren, they get it immediately,' observes Mel, his eyes reflecting the optimism of a child refusing to be buried under the fear that comes from limited frameworks of what's possible. Fortunately, he chose to be more irrational and less mediocre. If he hadn't, the world would be deprived of his beautiful legacy and everything that has been and will be built on it.

Social entrepreneurship may not be your arena, but the actions of learning, trusting, risking and changing are the same for you, as well as the starting point. Firstly, get clear on what goes fundamentally against the reality you want to see in your leadership landscape, even if it seems impossible and, quite honestly, irrational. Secondly, get ready to do something about it.

As Mel said to me: 'Just do what you do. You're helping right now, because – what do you do? You're a writer, so you're writing about it [my story]. You don't have to do anything else. What we do, our little contribution, is we take a ball to where homeless people are and say, "Do you want to play football?" That's it. That's all we do.'

Isn't it really that simple? All you must do is be ready to walk on the edge and be clear about why you're doing it.

Get started and connect

Sometimes, all you need to do is start – no matter how late, difficult, impossible, fill-in-the-gap you think it is for you. If you have any doubts about this, watch the film of a woman reaching the Florida shore after almost fifty-three hours of swimming in the ocean at the age of sixty-four, declaring, 'You're never too old to chase your dreams.'[101]

The next story is about Diana Nyad, someone I speak of often. Listening to one of her many speeches, I love to hear how she describes what I call a bold mind: 'Whatever your particular other shore is if you just don't quit, you will reach your other shore.'[102]

Her idea had already chosen her while she was still a little girl, and it's always been about more than just sport.[103] As she once said, it's about ways to live life. Ever since her childhood, she developed her relationship with this idea, and intensified it during the Cuban Revolution, which – as she remembers – made that place a mysterious location to everyone in South Florida. She recalls her mother pointing out towards Havana, telling her it was so close that she could almost swim there.

This is when the idea of doing exactly that selected Diana and she trusted it in her mind for many years to come.

In 1978, Diana Nyad made her first attempt to swim from Cuba to Florida, a distance of 103 miles through the Florida Straits. This body of water is known for its strong currents and unpredictable weather, as well as the presence of sharks and jellyfish. Nyad, then twenty-eight and already an accomplished marathon swimmer known for her open-water achievements such as a record-breaking swim around Manhattan, swam inside a shark cage for protection.

Despite her rigorous physical and mental preparation, Nyad faced numerous challenges during the swim, including adverse weather conditions and strong ocean currents. After swimming for about forty-two hours and covering a significant distance, she had to give up due to rough seas and exhaustion. At the time, this long-standing quest remained a dream; one she would famously achieve much later – in 2013 at the age of sixty-four.

By 2 September 2013, Nyad was a prominent sports broadcaster and journalist, but the idea had always been there, refusing to let go of her. On that day, she became the first person to swim from Cuba to Florida without the aid of a shark cage, swimming 110.86 miles in fifty-three hours from Havana to Key West. Before her attempt, she wondered if there was more to life than what she was experiencing. Her success likely confirmed that there was.

In her TED Talk, she quotes Socrates, 'To be is to do', to emphasise that there is action behind her words when she says, 'Don't ever give up.'[104] To never give up, you have to start first, but how can you start if you do not trust your idea? The second-best thing is to connect with those around you – which is what Diana did – ensuring they understand your level of trust in what you've started. Your bold idea may seem irrational to others, but once someone joins you, it becomes a story that's no longer just yours, and you're not the only one trusting it makes sense.

A decade later, reflecting on that life-changing adventure – life-changing not only for her but for the many inspired by her story – Diana noted that she and her team had attempted the crossing more than once, facing intense challenges from nature. Their success was a shared achievement, demonstrating, as she put it, that 'as with every one of life's imposing endeavours, it's never one person who succeeds alone.'[105] That's one of the messages she delivered, swollen and exhausted, when she touched the no-water ground at Key West: 'It looks like a solitary sport, but it takes a team.'[106]

Far less physically, emotionally or logistically demanding walks on the edge still require a team. No one does it alone. Regardless of the power of her individual perseverance, Diana Nyad recalls the moment when Bonnie – her best friend and head handler responsible for managing the entire support team – grabbed her shoulders and said, 'Let's find our way to Florida.' When you start and connect with others, your path becomes a shared one and, depending on the nature of your journey, that can be the only way to reach your destination.

Before her success, there were moments when sports scientists and other experts, and even her own team including Bonnie, were convinced that it was an impossible adventure. Nonetheless, Bonnie offered Diana her full support, stating that if Diana was determined to follow her idea, she'd be beside her to the end. That's wonderful, but we don't always have that level of support.

Here comes the paradox: while it's almost contrary to nature to do anything so important alone, you need to give yourself permission to be your own hero in your walk on the edge, if that's what it takes to continue. That means not giving up even when everyone else has. Enrolling others into your vision is one thing. Holding your vision subject to the approval of others is quite another.

Diana Nyad is often asked a simple question – why? Why would anyone want to do that to herself? That's when she speaks about anything but sport, talking about how she wants to end her life without regrets.[107]

It's a choice. Instead of talking yourself out of your bold idea, your agency, your walk on the edge, which is so easy to do, you simply find a way. During an interview she gave to CNN's Sanjay Gupta, Diana didn't hide away from the fact that it's hard: 'Even people with iron will quit when it's really tough.'[108] If your idea is important to you, though, you can choose to stay with the challenge instead of talking yourself out of it. One of these choices is easier in the moment; the other is easier to live with.

In that same interview, while her face and mouth were still swollen from her swim, making it difficult for her to speak, she talked about what helped sustain her. It was her own monologue while in the ocean: 'Forget about the surface up. Get your hands in somehow and with your left hand push Cuba back and push Florida toward you.' There comes a moment when walking on the edge towards our vision is a matter of grit and discipline – two things that can be staunch allies to our great mind and such a powerful antidote to our safe one.

There were some controversies after Diana's achievement, as there always will be, about whether she did everything according to sports rules. While she stood her ground in terms of official sports regulations, she made it clear that her arena was much larger than the sports arena. Swimming for fifty-two hours and fifty-four minutes at the age of sixty-four – is there anyone who thinks this is merely about breaking a world record?

Over a decade later, she remains true to her message, her mission, her fundamental choice. Completing and celebrating what she has created, Diana has dedicated herself to EverWalk,[109] an initiative she established together with Bonnie to promote walking as a way to counteract sedentary lifestyles. EverWalk hosts epic walking events and reflects Diana Nyad's commitment to physical health. The world has witnessed how her edge walk showed a way of building character and movement – I'm not sure if one can survive without the other – and her story will remain part of my many keynotes to organisations as an answer to a too frequent mantra: it's too much, it's too late, it's too risky, it cannot be done.

Get real and bold

The two stories I'm about to share illustrate the extraordinary impact of individuals who, in moments of danger, with little time to think or rationalise, chose to take bold risks and seize their cubic centimetre of chance.

Taking risks is like swimming – you can't experience it from the shore; you must dive in, get real and bold, and swim. The first story reflects this analogy perfectly.

In 2015, two sisters fled war-torn Syria in search of a safer life in Europe. Their journey took them through Lebanon to Turkey, where they boarded a small, over-crowded inflatable boat heading to Greece. The boat, designed for far fewer than the twenty aboard, began taking on water shortly into the journey, spreading panic among the passengers.

Recognising the danger, the sisters made a courageous decision in an instant. Both being competitive swimmers, they knew they had the skills needed to help. Despite the waters being dark and cold, they jumped in to push and guide the boat towards the Greek shore – to safety. Two others jumped in to join them.

For over three and a half hours, they swam alongside the boat, pushing it through the water. Exhausted but determined, they managed to save themselves and their fellow passengers, including young children. Their extraordinary efforts brought everyone safely to the shores of Lesbos, Greece.

The second story, set in June 2018, also underscores the power of risk. When twelve boys from the Wild Boars football team and their assistant coach explored the Tham Luang cave in Chiang Rai province, Thailand, they encountered an unexpected disaster. The boys, aged eleven to sixteen, along with their twenty-five-year-old coach, were familiar with the cave, but heavy rainfall partially flooded it, trapping them inside.

When the boys didn't return home, their families informed the authorities, who found their bicycles and gear at the cave entrance. Rescue efforts began immediately, but were prevented by rising water levels. It took nine days to locate the boys approximately four kilometres from the entrance. The challenge then was to extract them from the narrow, dark submerged passageways.

An Australian anaesthetist and recreational cave diver belonged to an informal group that had taken on some of the world's deepest caves.[110] Technical cave diving is known as the Formula One of diving, and this group liked to push the limits of exploration in the most challenging environments. This anaesthetist was called in by the British diving team for his rare skills as a diver and medic who's used to working in extreme conditions.

When another diver on the team had the shocking idea to ask the Australian doctor to use anaesthetics to sedate the boys, preventing panic during their extraction, his answer was a clear no. Rationally, he did not believe that the plan could ever work, but in the next moment, he embraced the fact that this irrational suggestion was the only one, given the circumstances, that made sense. He decided to take a risk.

The meticulously planned rescue operation lasted three days, beginning on 8 July 2018. Each boy was fitted with a full-face diving mask, sedated, and then escorted by expert divers through the flooded passages. The journey took several hours for each boy, requiring precise coordination. By 10 July 2018, all twelve boys and their coach had been successfully rescued.

The first story is about Sara and Yusra Mardini.[111] Yusra went on to compete in the 2016 Olympics in Rio as part of the Refugee Olympic Team, drawing international attention to the topic of refugees and the remarkable strength of the human spirit. The second one is about Dr Richard 'Harry' Harris who, together with his friend and fellow diving team member Dr Craig Challen, was awarded Australian of the Year in 2019 for his heroic efforts.[112]

Harris's experience has expanded his arena, turning him into an author, filmmaker, public speaker and a huge advocate for embracing risk. In his book *The Art of Risk*, he explores the stories of other people who regularly risk their lives and invites us to learn from their expertise.[113] Dr Richard Harris's decision to take that particular risk had an unmistakable impact: it was a cubic centimetre of chance moment that ultimately saved thirteen people from what seemed like certain death.

Both stories feature individuals who took the lead in a critical moment. They made a call and embraced the risk, and that risk saved lives. With their head, heart and gut, they knew they had to step up, take charge and seize their cubic centimetre of chance to make a difference. There was no time for lengthy debates or rationalisation.

Seizing your cubic centimetre of chance is about being real and bold in the moment. Right now. It's about courageously declaring that you know what you're doing, because part of you genuinely does.

As I was writing this section, one of my clients called. She's an exceptionally capable woman running her own small business, yet she's struggled to realise her full potential. She'd been holding back for years, but now, she's become clear on the investment she wants to make to elevate her business according to her vision. It's a significant investment for her – an amaz-ing step – and she's decided to go for it.

'I just wanted to check with you,' she said. 'I'm about to take this massive risk. I think it's what I need to do, but part of me is terrified; my bones are shaking. Is this what a real, serious risk feels like?'

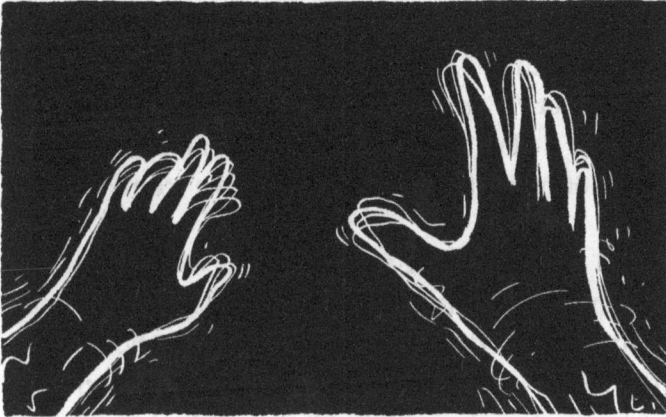

I could sense both thrill and terror in her voice and that's exactly how it feels. Even if you're not in physi-cal danger, your head, heart and gut still react as if you are when you're about to take a risk that scares you. The one that's irrational from so many aspects, yet feels so right, your very bones can sense it.

If they could speak, they'd say in sheer terror, 'Hold on tight, s/he's doing it.' Regardless of your leadership landscape, if you think you're walking on the edge, showing up real and bold in your arena, but have never felt your bones shake, you're probably not.

Complete and celebrate

Imagine one of the richest nations in the world where, despite its immense wealth, over 14 million people still live in poverty. In the UK, around 20% of the population, including 4.2 million children, struggle to make ends meet.[114] Now picture someone bold enough to propose a plan to end this issue within five years – a proposition that might easily provoke scepticism.

Helen Rowe received acclaim for doing just that, refusing to normalise poverty or blame it on individuals' poor decisions. In our conversation, Helen recalled a pivotal moment in a conversation with a decision maker while she was working at the Housing Association.

'As a society, we have run out of ideas,' the decision maker said. 'We just don't know what to do.'

I guess that's when her idea selected her. That statement lingered with her, especially after she became a mother, giving her the time to reflect deeply. Faced with societal failures, she could either be consumed by anger or use her skills to spark change. Drawing from her experience at the Foreign Office, where she had created significant papers for the government, she realised her contribution.

'I'm not a multimillionaire or anything; I can't suddenly create a philanthropic society, but I can write. That's where it all began.'

That was the start of *Eliminating Poverty in Britain*, a book that explores the socio-economic and health impacts of poverty.[115] Published in 2023, it offers a plan to eradicate poverty within five years without increasing taxes. Does it sound like an irrational idea?

Helen has used extensive research and real-life narratives to illustrate the widespread consequences of poverty on mental and physical health, communities and the economy. Recognising that politicians often lack the time to dive deeply into these issues, once the book was published, she focused on connecting with civil service and frontline professionals – those who can directly influence change. Her book has been praised for its insightful analysis and practical solutions, with Jo Brand, a British comedian, writer, presenter and actress, commending it for providing 'a wealth of new ideas to begin to mend us'.[116]

After completing her significant work, Helen claimed a new arena, bringing together her knowledge of biology and social science. She recognised that no solution, regardless of its thoroughness and clarity, would be effective unless accompanied by a shift in perspective. This led her to the creation of a transformative training programme, The Biology of Poverty,[117] where she teaches how living in poverty can impact

individuals down to their DNA, and how addressing poverty can improve everyone's quality of life, no
matter their financial status.

'I'm really trying to embed compassion back into our
society through biological knowledge and understanding of how it [poverty] affects the human body,'
she explained to me passionately, marking the beginning of another bold initiative.

These people's stories, presented at various stages of
their quest, are all different, but from a certain perspective, they share a common element: the presence
of irrationality at the very core of the idea itself. All
these ideas could easily have been dismissed not only
by others, but also by their creators, but they were not.

That's because these bold people are not about being
irrational; they're about refusing to settle for mediocrity.
That's what we all achieve by being leaders on the edge.
As a reminder, leading on the edge doesn't mean waiting at the edge in passivity, distance or drive, but actively
walking on it in action, on a quest, while, of course,
embracing all the discomfort that this choice brings.

If you read between the lines of their stories, you'll
see that all these leaders understand their profit – it's
the difference they make for themselves and others.
They are clear about what they intend to do with their
lives. They are not being crazy; they are taking seriously the notion that changing the world is the sum

of a billion tiny sparks, and some of these sparks must come from them.

In the 2018 documentary *Robin Williams: Come inside my mind*, which features extensive footage and personal interviews with this amazing actor and artist, there is a scene in which he's inviting us to be crazy: 'It's too late to be sane. You're only given a little spark of madness, and if you lose that, you're nothing.'[118] It's too late *not* to lead on the edge. Doing so, you are far from being nothing. In fact, there are lots of moments when, to yourself, many others and the world, you are everything.

Epilogue

Many of you may be eager to know what happened next in my own story; what the outcome has been of my world on the edge. After thirteen years in the justice system – waiting for key witnesses, navigating a maze of cases designed to sidetrack us – my husband and I finally won the court ruling in our favour. Around the same time, another long-standing case, which had often been used as a diversion from the core issue, but was still legally crucial, was reconfirmed once again in our favour after six years, this time with the Supreme Court rejecting the appeal and therefore its revision.

This entire saga could fill a book of its own. In fact, I intend to work with a legal expert and author to document the full story. My aim is to provide legal clarity and offer emotional empowerment through this story for anyone facing or considering a similar walk on the edge. This is one way I intend to build on my legacy – a path that has crystallised for me – but I sense intuitively that there are other paths emerging beyond this one. When the time is right, these will become clear as well.

There's something else about my walk on the edge that I want to emphasise here. When these court rulings came through in my favour, I found a part of me struggling to accept them, struggling to embrace the change that had occurred, as though I was afraid there would be more and this was not yet the closing arc of this particular journey. Taking the time to sit with this fearful part of myself in a session with my brilliant coach of many years, I realised it was an old story, a helpless identity. It's the part in some dark little corner of me that, though it knows it has been standing and will continue to stand up against the abuse of power, still doubts whether it will ultimately make any difference. Can real change truly happen? Is walking on this edge done?

Sometimes, completing and celebrating walking on the edge is as demanding as being in the middle of it. It requires us to shed the old and allow the new to take root – to replace the dead cells within us with fresh ones. Until the very last moment and beyond, we need to keep remembering how bold we are at the cellular level, at the core of our body's wisdom, before layers of lived experiences, family upbringing, societal and cultural shaping seeking to prove other-wise settle in and call themselves 'identity'.

For me, this requires embracing the sense of ease, recognising that the long, hard work is done. There comes a time when we need to let lightness in, to make way for the next bold – perhaps irrational – initiative. I'll keep you posted in my future books. For now, I'll close with the words of Marcus Aurelius: 'The universe is change. Life is opinion.'[119]

Why these words? Because of the deep realisation one inevitably gains while walking on the edge: change is unstoppable. Completing and celebrating are not the end of change, but the beginning of a new arc of transformation. Life as opinion simply reminds us to take each walk on the edge and its stages with a bit of ease, whether we're at the beginning, middle or the end. As the saying goes, take it light, but take it.

KEY IDEAS

On the Quest is a four-step roadmap for daring on the edge, pursuing bold self-discovery and achieving extraordinary change for a better world:

1. **Get clear and ready:** begin with the learning process to clarify your purpose and prepare for bold action.

---

2. **Get started and connect**: trust your idea
    and take the first step, building meaningful
    connections to support your journey.

3. **Get real and bold**: take a decisive risk that
    pushes boundaries and creates a pivotal moment
    of change.

4. **Complete and celebrate**: reflect on the impact
    you've achieved, celebrate the success and
    prepare to embark on your next bold quest.

Your mirror moment

We all have the power to inspire. Unlock it; step into
the shoes of extraordinary leaders whose stories have
been told, reflect deeply and take the leap – leaving
mediocrity behind.

1. Are you on a quest or are you simply playing
    it safe by ignoring your boldest ideas? Mel
    Young transformed a simple conversation
    into the Homeless World Cup. What could
    you accomplish if you stopped settling for
    good enough?

2. Why keep accepting what makes no sense? Helen
    Rowe refused to see poverty as unsolvable.
    What radical move will you make to disrupt the
    status quo?

3. How often do you let doubt kill your brilliance? Yusra Mardini didn't. What must you do to let your brilliance shine through?

4. Why wait for validation? Diana Nyad swam from Cuba to Florida despite the doubts of the people around her. Are you ready to lead, even if no one else believes in your idea?

5. Who could amplify your bold idea? Mel Young built a global network for the Homeless World Cup. Who do you need to bring on board?

6. What's your 'other shore'? Diana Nyad pursued hers against all odds. Is fear just a sign you're on the right path?

7. What risks are you avoiding that could be game-changers? Dr Richard Harris made a risky decision to save the lives of twelve boys and their football coach. What bold step of yours could have an extraordinary impact?

8. What change will you celebrate when your idea becomes real, like Helen Rowe's radical plan to end poverty? How will you make your legacy a daring solution, not a safe option?

NINE

What Are You Trying To Do?

*S*ervant Leadership by Robert K Greenleaf gives us another thought-provoking question – what are you trying to do? – saying it's one of the easiest questions to ask and one of the most difficult to answer.[120] I'll try to give an answer for myself by recalling one of the episodes from my childhood.

I remember him vividly; at times, I thought he was the most intelligent person in the world. He often visited our house for coffee and conversation – my parents also held him in high regard, considering him a lifelong friend. I'll refer to him as Mr M.

My parents had their fair share of challenges and Mr M was a steadfast supporter in a number of ways. I loved our conversations. Being a diligent student all my life with learning as one of my core values, I found common ground with Mr M and he frequently praised my academic results. I was impressed by his life energy and his adaptability in his dynamic career path, from being a pilot at a young age to starting a factory in his sixties and having many other roles in between, and I deeply trusted his brilliant mind.

Once, we were discussing my future and I mentioned my intention to study English, a decision I made when I was quite young. I saw mastering English as my doorway to experiencing the world. My motives differed from my mother's expectations – she envisioned the regular hours of a schoolteacher as suitable for my potential future roles as a mother and wife. I'm not entirely sure she believed in that scenario herself, but one thing I've learned is that the need for security can make us accept our most unlikely narratives.

Reflecting on it now, I wonder why Mr M didn't challenge my decision with some wise advice, considering he knew my true motives. Perhaps he simply trusted that things would naturally align with my career choice, which I believe they did.

In any case, aware of my intentions, he showed up at our house shortly afterwards with a gift – a comprehensive English dictionary. I was thrilled. Inside the front cover was a message, succinct yet profound: 'Whatever you choose to do, don't be mediocre.' At the age of eleven, I didn't know what mediocre meant, so I asked him. He suggested that my mother would explain it, perhaps thinking of how she and my father embodied anything but mediocrity, given their journey from challenging beginnings to their achievements. However, not satisfied with her explanation, Mr M intervened to clarify and the conversation went into the nuances of mediocrity. I eventually tuned out, lost in my own thoughts.

As I began to understand the meaning of the word, I realised he had left me with a phrase that resonated deeply. Perhaps due to my mother's presence, he omitted mentioning that following such advice comes with its risks. I suppose he believed that if I truly embraced this guidance in my life and work, I would eventually figure that out on my own.

The sin of mediocrity

Every life has the potential to be extraordinary until the individual living it decides otherwise. In today's world, which calls for anything but the ordinary, making that decision comes at a high cost, which is what Dawna Markova, American author, psychologist and researcher, speaks about when she says she refuses to 'die an unlived life'.[121]

Besides an unlived life, there is also the price of untapped leadership. Imagine a leader who has never really tapped into their own full potential. This image,

I hope, will encourage you to pause and reflect on the choices you have been making.

I meet so many remarkable leaders in my arena and hear their exceptional stories. While each is unique, a recurring theme is risk. It's disheartening to continually observe how the biggest obstacle to human greatness is the obsessive avoidance of risk – the repeated deliberate choice to lead nothing more than a safe, ordinary life.

We all know it is human nature to favour the well-known path defined by predictability because it protects us from the unknown, which seems unsafe, but do we really need such protection at all costs, and is the unknown genuinely that unsafe? Before we even begin to ask ourselves these questions, this mindset dilutes our dreams and turns our aspirations into a foggy haze, leaving us with nothing but a faint image of what might have been our bold potential. This image reminds us that we have failed to recognise the power we naturally hold and the responsibility that accompanies it.

This is a sophisticated way to describe the impact of the deceptive taste of the ordinary. Unlike that, the pursuit of the extraordinary is accompanied by uncertainty. No uncertainty, no extraordinariness – that's the deal. Uncertainty is an inescapable part of progress.

Every time I give a keynote and ask leaders, 'How many of you like making a difference in your leadership landscape?', an avalanche of hands goes up. 'How many of you like taking risks?' The number of hands is noticeably fewer.

However, making a difference comes with risks. It involves risking the security of the known and embracing the uncertainty of change. It asks you to let go of the safety nets that have cushioned you: your 'common sense' that has been diligently safeguarding you; the functional roles you have meticulously carved; your reputations that you have cultivated; and sometimes even the financial stability that you have sacrificed much to build.

All these elements suddenly find themselves juxtaposed against the uncertainty inherent in any extraordinary goal and meaningful change that your true leadership potential is craving. While these safety nets are creating resistance to change, pushing you back into the realms of the familiar, the safe and secure, the ordinary, you forget to ask what if? What if the unknown holds much greater potential for you and your leadership landscape?

In this dance between bold aspiration and rational hesitation, between your soul's hunger for impact and your rational mind's fear of the unknown, you'll find the paradox that defines your leadership and your life. That paradox holds an invitation for all of us to resist the comfort of subscribing to an ordinary life. It's that simple really. If we could just risk an ordinary life for the sake of an extraordinary world – and when I say extraordinary world, I mean the extraordinary landscape in which we lead – we wouldn't need to worry about the rest. The rest would get sorted out by somebody making the same risky choice as us.

We are all chosen by our ideas, chosen for extraordinary leadership. I'm inspired by Martha Graham, considered a pioneer of modern dance who played with the expressive capacity of the human body in an extraordinary way, continuing to dance into her seventies and creating dances well into her nineties. When asked why she chose to be a dancer, she said: 'I did not choose. I was chosen to be a dancer, and with that, you live all your life.'[122]

Why are we making it so hard to embrace what has chosen us? Why don't we decide to listen to those screams of our fundamental choice, bring that spark to our leadership landscape, feel that passion for the arenas that are ours, hear that resolute voice inviting us to do something about it, partner with that irrational idea that doesn't seem to be leaving us, get on that boat whose horn relentlessly blares in front of our window before it gets tired of us and leaves?

Why? Not? Do? Just? That? You'll save your bold soul from losing its aliveness, and yourself from committing the only sin Martha Graham says there is:

mediocrity. Then, whatever it is you're trying to do, you'll make a real difference.

KEY IDEAS

- What are you trying to do? This is the hardest question you must answer.
- Know that your ordinary choices kill your extraordinary potential.
- No risk, no progress, no greatness.
- Bold ideas choose you – don't ignore them.
- Let go of safety to rise beyond mediocrity.

Your mirror moment

Stop hiding behind mediocrity. Start daring.

1. What are you going to do – really?

Your activation zone

- List your top three game-changing ideas from Part 3.
- Where, how and when will you apply these ideas?
- What will happen if you don't take action?

Conclusion

I have shared many stories in this book. My intention is to make it clear that the most important one is the story you continue to tell yourself about yourself and your world.

Otto Scharmer, a senior lecturer at MIT and founding chair of the Presencing Institute who has spent many years helping leaders embrace personal and social transformation, offers a powerful perspective on this.[123] He explains that two narratives are playing out in the world today: the first is one of destruction, loss and fear; the second is a story of possibility, hope and the beginning of profound regeneration. He calls this second story the most important and least well-told story of our time.

I mentioned Otto Scharmer earlier in this book, high-lighting his view that humanity's greatest challenge is our belief in our lack of agency to address the crises we face. I concluded that while we are fully capable of creating the change we wish to see, we are often unready to dare to take the necessary steps.

Our constant question of *how* reveals our reluctance to dare. How do we hear that inner voice, find our spark, define our vision? How do we feel passion, trust, take risks, walk on the edge? How do we lead? How do we live?

That information is already in your soul. If you're not hearing it, perhaps it's time to pause and listen to the silence. Confront your deepest fears – they may be layered over your dreams of change. Dig deep, trust what you find, then get exposed and share your vision of change with someone to start making it real. Sit in the fire of transformation as long as it takes, reshaping yourself and your world. Keep repeating this cycle, activating your soul to bring forth what it's meant to. How? By daring.

Being ready to dare means choosing to tell the story of possibility with more conviction than ever before. I urge you to dare to speak your irrational idea out loud, to initiate the bold conversation and to commit to following through even after you've slept on it. Keep risking your significance for the difference you can make.

You know you have the idea because it has chosen you. Listen to it, embrace it and take it forward in your landscape, your organisation, your family, your community. Whatever skills you may lack, you'll find ways to acquire them along the way, once you take seriously the one thing that sets you apart as a leader and an extraordinary individual: your sense of agency – your power and responsibility to create change.

Let this book and the stories within it inspire you. Choose to activate yourself. Learn to gain clarity and readiness, trust in your ability to start and connect with others, and risk being real and bold. Then celebrate the important meaningful change that occurs because you dared.

Robin Arzón, ultramarathoner and the author of the *New York Times* bestseller *Shut Up and Run*,[124] has made it her life's mission to redefine and rethink possibility through movement. Similarly, leaders must redefine and rethink possibility through bold action, which is the foundation of all progress. Arzón says, 'There's no room for mediocre yeses. It's either a "hell yes" or a "no, thank you".'

This principle holds true in leadership– though sadly, many have convinced themselves otherwise. Now you've read this book, don't let it gather dust on a shelf. Keep returning to it whenever you need to reignite your conviction to tell a different story – the one that reflects a resounding "hell yes" to what your work in the world is. Then, alert and present, ask yourself:

What are you going to do, really?

You've always known your choice is to be so much more than mediocre.

Let's lead the change together

If you're ready to keep this bold conversation going and seek more inspiration and activation, we can partner to make great things happen. As a published author, keynote speaker and bold leadership coach, I've had the privilege of supporting leaders and organisations in transformative ways. While many moments stand out, each experience reinforces one truth: it's the courage to take bold steps that leads to real transformation.

To explore what's possible for your organisation, here's how we can work together:

- **Keynote**: I deliver engaging and actionable talks that inspire audiences to embrace change and take bold action.

- **Partner for leadership development**: with tailored programmes and tools like the Leadership Circle Profile® and the SOUL

Framework®, I help leaders and teams
achieve meaningful growth and cultivate
bold leadership.

Let's bring transformative conversations to your
organisation and unlock the full potential of your
leadership landscape. Together, we can lead an
extraordinary change.

Notes

1   O Scharmer, E Pomeroy, 'Fourth person: The knowing of the field', *Journal of Awareness-Based Systems Change*, 4/1 (2024), 19–48, https://jabsc.org/index.php/jabsc/article/view/7909/6699

2   R Federer, Commencement Address at Dartmouth (2024), www.youtube.com/watch?v=pqWUuYTcG-o, accessed 26 October 2024

3   G MacKenzie, *Orbiting the Giant Hairball: A corporate fool's guide to surviving with grace* (Viking, 1998)

4   Z Goic Petricevic, *Bold Reinvented: Next level leading with courage, consciousness and conviction* (Bold Leadership Culture, 2021)

5   S Altman, featured in '25 Thinkers for a world on the brink', *Prospect Magazine* (January/February 2024), www.prospectmagazine.co.uk/world/63099/25-thinkers-for-a-world-on-the-brink, accessed 26 October 2024

6   The World's Top Thinkers, '25 Thinkers for a world on the brink', *Prospect Magazine* (January/February 2024), www.prospectmagazine.co.uk/world/63099/25-thinkers-for-a-world-on-the-brink, accessed 26 October 2024

7   Ibid

8 Our World in Data, Conflict Data Explorer, https://ourworldindata.org/explorers/conflict-data, accessed 26 October 2024

9 United Nations High Commissioner for Refugees (UNHCR), Global Trends: Forced Displacement, www.unhcr.org/global-trends-report-2023, accessed 26 October 2024

10 Homeless World Cup (no date), www.homelessworldcup.org/impact, accessed 3 February 2025

11 Internal Displacement Monitoring Centre (IDMC), Global Report on Internal Displacement 2024, https://api.internal-displacement.org/sites/default/files/publications/documents/IDMC-GRID-2024-Global-Report-on-Internal-Displacement.pdf, accessed 26 October 2024

12 *The Letter*, directed by Nicolas Brown (2022), YouTube, www.youtube.com/watch?v=Rps9bs85BII, accessed 26 October 2024

13 RMIT University, 'Clean energy tech extracts power from ocean waves', *RMIT University News* (11 August 2021), www.rmit.edu.au/news/all-news/2021/aug/wave-energy-technology, accessed 26 October 2024

14 Masaka Kids Africana, Home, www.masakakidsafricana.com, accessed 26 October 2024

15 A Corbley, 'Millionaire builds 99 tiny homes to cut homelessness in his community – He even provides jobs on site for them', *Good News Network* (30 October 2023), www.goodnewsnetwork.org/millionaire-builds-99-tiny-homes-to-cut-homelessness-in-his-community-he-even-provides-jobs-on-site-for-them, accessed 26 October 2024

16 JA Jacobs, K Gerson, *The Time Divide: Work, family, and gender inequality* (Harvard University Press, 2004)

17 YN Harari, *21 Lessons for the 21st Century* (Jonathan Cape, 2018)

18 K Morgan, 'Why we define ourselves by our jobs', *BBC Worklife* (13 April 2021), www.bbc.com/worklife/article/20210409-why-we-define-ourselves-by-our-jobs, accessed 26 October 2024

19 Pope John Paul II, *Laborem Exercens: Encyclical letter on human work* (Vatican, 1981), https://christusliberat.org/journal/laborem-exercens-encyclical-letter-on-human-work-pope-john-paul-ii, accessed 26 October 2024

20 H Ibarra, *Working Identity: Unconventional strategies for reinventing your career* (Harvard Business Review Press, 2003), p3 Kindle Edition

21 T McKenna, 'Nature loves courage', YouTube (2019) www.youtube.com/watch?v=NMR--VXFyGA, accessed 8 January 2025

22 L Smith, 'Why you will fail to have a great career', TEDxUW, 2011, www.youtube.com/watch?v=iKHTawgyKWQ, accessed 26 October 2024

23 C Gallo, *Talk Like TED: The 9 public-speaking secrets of the world's top minds* (St Martin's Press, 2014)

24 K Ilicic, Kristijan Ilicic Travel Experiences, www.kristijanilicic.com, accessed 26 October 2024

25 M Noroc, *The Atlas of Beauty: Women of the world in 500 portraits* (Ten Speed Press, 2017)

26 M Noroc, *The Power of Women* (Penguin, March 2025)

27 Gallup, *State of the Global Workplace: 2024 Report*, Gallup Inc, 2024

28 RJ Anderson, *The Spirit of Leadership* (Leadership Circle®, 2021) https://leadershipcircle.com/wp-content/uploads/2021/07/Spirit-of-Leadership-Whitepaper-2021-07.pdf, accessed 2 January 2025

29 H Keller, 'Inspirational quote by Helen Keller', Coachability Foundation, www.coachabilityfoundation.org/post/inspirational-quote-by-helen-keller-1, accessed 26 October 2024

30 Designed Learning official website, www.designedlearning.com, accessed 26 October 2024

31 CRR Global, Organisation and Relationship Systems Coaching (ORSC), www.crrglobal.com, accessed 26 October 2024

32 M Heffernan, 'Forget the pecking order at work', TED, 2015, www.ted.com/talks/margaret_heffernan_forget_the_pecking_order_at_work?subtitle=en, accessed 26 October 2024

33 Gallup, *State of the Global Workplace: 2024 Report*, Gallup Inc, 2024

34 Gallup, *State of the Global Workplace: 2024 Report*, Gallup Inc, 2024

35 K Mulligan, LinkedIn profile, www.linkedin.com/in/kathleenmulligannewwaveleadership, accessed 26 October 2024

36 Z Petricevic, 'The game of change: How to be a bold player' (no date), www.zanagoicpetricevic.com, accessed 3 February 2025

37 A Lindgren, *Pippi Longstocking*, trans. by Oxford University Press (Oxford University Press, 1954), first published as Pippi Långstrump by Rabén and Sjögren, 1945

38 N Sangwan, 'Understanding, preventing & healing burnout with Dr Neha Sangwan', *Warrior's Day Off*, Season 4, Episode 6, https://podcasts.apple.com/us/podcast/understanding-preventing-healing-burnout-with-dr-neha/id1539158764?i=1000657910021, accessed 26 October 2024

39 PB Vaill, *Learning as a Way of Being: Strategies for survival in a world of permanent white water* (Jossey-Bass, 1996)

40 PwC, 26th Annual Global CEO Survey (2023), www.pwc.com/gx/en/ceo-survey/2023/main/download/26th_CEO_Survey_PDF_v1.pdf, accessed 26 October 2024

41 J Foster, 'Insights at the edge', *Life Without A Centre* podcast (2012), www.lifewithoutacentre.com/interviews-articles/insights-at-the-edge-interview-with-jeff-foster-transcript, accessed 26 October 2024

42 CRR Global, ORSC: Organisation and Relationship Systems Coaching Methodology, www.crrglobal.com, accessed 26 October 2024

43 R Fritz, *The Path of Least Resistance: Principles for creating what you want to create* (DMA, 1984), p106

44 R Fritz, *The Path of Least Resistance*, p109

45 *Queen of the Desert*, directed by Werner Herzog (IFC Films, 2015)

46 RJ Anderson, 'Leadership: Uncommon Sense', Leadership Circle (2018), https://leadershipcircle.com/wp-content/uploads/2018/03/Leadership-Uncommon-Sense-Whitepaper-MARCH2017.pdf, accessed 3 February 2025

47 NS Nye, *Missing the Boat*, in *You and Yours* (BOA Editions, 2005)

48 Inner Development Goals, 'Inner Development Goals film', YouTube (2021), www.youtube.com/watch?v=xsB5ci-rgGg, accessed 29 January 2025

49 Ibid

50 Inner Development Goals, https://innerdevelopmentgoals.org, accessed 26 October 2024

51 United Nations, The 17 Goals, https://sdgs.un.org/goals, accessed 12 January 2025

52 Leadership Circle®, Leadership Circle Profile®, Integrating the field of leadership with the most comprehensive 360° leadership assessment, www.leadershipcircle.com

53 Leadership Circle®, *Profile Interpretation Manual*, Version 2022.1, https://leadershipcircle.com/wp-content/uploads/2022/07/LCP-Interpretation-Manual-VIRTUAL--v2022.1.pdf, accessed 1 February 2025

54 R Sharma, *The Wealth Money Can't Buy: The 8 hidden habits to live your richest life* (Crown, 2024)

55 S Godin, 'Unaware', Seth's Blog (27 January 2024), https://seths.blog/2024/01/unaware, accessed 29 January 2025

56 B Anderson, B Adams, *Reactive to Creative Leadership* (Leadership Circle®, 3 August 2017), p3, https://leadershipcircle.com/wp-content/uploads/2019/01/Reactive-to-Creative-Leadership_edit.pdf, accessed 7 January 2025

57 J Hollis, *Finding Meaning in the Second Half of Life: How to finally really grow up* (Gotham Books, 2006)

58 R Goffee, G Jones, 'Why should anyone be led by you?', *Harvard Business Review*, 78/5 (2000), https://hbr.org/2000/09/why-should-anyone-be-led-by-you, accessed 26 October 2024

59 SD Friedman, AF Westring, *Parents Who Lead: The leadership approach you need to parent with purpose, fuel your career, and create a richer life* (Harvard Business Review Press, 2020)

60 SD Friedman, 'Define your personal leadership vision', *Harvard Business Review*, (2008), https://hbr.org/2008/08/title, accessed 26 October 2024

61 Z Goic Petricevic, *Bold Reinvented*

62 Leadership Development, Günter Westphal website, https://guenterwestphal.com/leadership-development, accessed 27 October 2024

63 JJ Scherer, 'You don't have to change yourself. You need to come home to yourself. And that changes everything', Best Graduation Speeches, www.bestgraduationspeeches.com/john-jacob-scherer-commencement-speech, accessed 27 October 2024

64 C Gallo, *Talk Like TED: The 9 public-speaking secrets of the world's top minds* (St Martin's Press, 2014)

65 S Jobs, *Steve Jobs: The Lost Interview*, director Paul Sen, 2011

66 A Duckworth, *Grit: The power of passion and perseverance* (Scribner, 2016)

67 Z Ziglar, 'Character, Commitment, and Discipline', Ziglar (no date), www.ziglar.com/quotes/character-commitment-and-discipline, accessed 29 January 2025

68 S David, 'Embracing the contradiction of bothness', *Susan David Newsletter* (12 December 2023), www.susandavid. com/newsletter/embracing-the-contradiction-of-bothness, accessed 26 October 2024

69 Ibid

70 Under Armour, 'The only way is through' (Under Armour about page, January 2020), https://about.underarmour. com/en-us/stories/2020/01/the-only-way-is-through-. html, accessed 19 February 2025

71 'Lejla Zalihić, a heroic woman: She jumped into a flood, swam three kilometers, and saved her daughter', *Sarajevo Times* (6 October 2024), https://sarajevotimes.com/ lejla-zalihic-a-heroic-woman-she-jumped-into-a-flood-swam-three-kilometers-and-saved-her-daughter, accessed 26 October 2024

72 N James, 'Women this week: French athletes prohibited from playing in hijab for 2024 Olympic Games', Council on Foreign Relations (blog post, 29 September 2023), www. cfr.org/blog/women-week-french-athletes-prohibited-playing-hijab-2024-olympic-games, accessed 7 January 2025

73 Olympic Games Paris 2024, The Mascot (Olympics.com), https://olympics.com/en/olympic-games/paris-2024/ mascot?os=app&ref=app, accessed 26 October 2024

74 UniCredit Group, 'UniCredit Foundation advances educational support with multidimensional UCF Edu-Fund Platform', UniCredit press release (22 July 2024), www. unicreditgroup.eu/en/press-media/press-releases/2024/ july/unicredit-foundation-advances-educational-support-with-multidime.html, accessed 26 October 2024

75 S Do Couto, 'Patagonia's billionaire founder gives away company to fight climate change', *Global News* (15 September 2022),https://globalnews.ca/news/9131134/ patagonia-founder-yvon-chouinard-gives-away-company-climate-change, accessed 19 February 2025

76 B Sheppard et al, *Ten Years to Midnight: Four urgent global crises and their strategic solutions* (Berrett-Koehler, 2020)

77 Korn Ferry, 'Leadership is evolving. Are you?', www. kornferry.com/insights/featured-topics/leadership/ evolution-of-leadership, accessed 26 October 2024

78 Nike, 'Winning isn't for everyone: Am I a bad person?', YouTube (2024), www.youtube.com/ watch?v=pwLergHG81c, accessed 26 October 2024

79 O Burkeman, *Four Thousand Weeks: Time management for mortals* (Farrar, Straus and Giroux, 2021)

80 Z Goic Petricevic, *Bold Reinvented*

81 Profile Interpretation Manual, Leadership Circle®, Version 2022.1, https://leadershipcircle.com/wp-content/uploads/2022/07/LCP-Interpretation-Manual-VIRTUAL--v2022.1.pdf, accessed 1 February 2025

82 Leadership Circle Profile® is created and owned by Leadership Circle®, www.leadershipcircle.com

83 United Nations, Sustainable Development Goals, https://sdgs.un.org/goals, accessed 27 October 2024

84 A Gorman, 'Address to the United Nations', YouTube (2022), www.youtube.com/watch?v=ol6NmbU47Sk, accessed 27 October 2024

85 B Anderson, 'Leadership: Uncommon sense', LC White Paper Series (Leadership Circle®, 2017), https://leadershipcircle.com/wp-content/uploads/2018/03/Leadership-Uncommon-Sense-Whitepaper-MARCH2017.pdf, accessed 7 January 2025

86 B Zander, 'Zander at Davos, 2009: Happy Birthday!', YouTube (2009), www.youtube.com/watch?v=M8DaPQyvJ8Y, accessed 29 January 2025

87 MC Maultsby Jr, *Rational Behavior Therapy* (Prentice Hall, 1984)

88 E Gilbert, *Eat Pray Love: One woman's search for everything* (Bloomsbury, 2007)

89 O Scharmer, E Pomeroy, 'Fourth Person: The knowing of the field', *Journal of Awareness-Based Systems Change*, 4/1 (2024) 19–48, https://doi.org/10.47061/jasc.v4i1.7909, accessed 27 October 2024

90 Leadership Circle Profile®, The Authenticity Dimension, *LCP Manual*, p19, https://leadershipcircle.com/wp-content/uploads/2022/07/LCP-Interpretation-Manual-VIRTUAL-v2022.1.pdf, accessed 7 January 2025

91 A Seale, 'The Three Intelligences: Gateway to inner wisdom', Transformational Presence (2023), https://alanseale.substack.com/p/the-three-intelligences, accessed 27 October 2024

92 C Castaneda, *Tales of Power*, Kindle Edition (Atria Books, 2013)

93 Ibid

94 The American Presidency Project, 'Undelivered Address Prepared for Jefferson Day', 13 April 1945 (no date),

www.presidency.ucsb.edu/node/210105, accessed
29 January 2025

95 *Father Stu*, directed by Rosalind Ross (Sony Pictures, 2022)

96 RK Greenleaf, *Servant Leadership: A journey into the nature
of legitimate power and greatness* (25th Anniversary Edition,
Paulist Press, 2002), p23

97 R Fritz, *The Path of Least Resistance*

98 Homeless World Cup, https://homelessworldcup.org,
accessed 27 October 2024

99 *The Beautiful Game*, directed by Thea Sharrock (Netflix,
2024)

100 Homeless World Cup (no date), www.homelessworldcup.
org/impact, accessed 3 February 2025

101 *Nyad*, directed by Elizabeth Chai Vasarhelyi and Jimmy
Chin (Netflix, 2023)

102 National FFA Organization, 'Keynote: Diana Nyad – 89th
National FFA Convention & Expo' (2016), YouTube, www.
youtube.com/watch?v=id2Q_TpgAx4&t=1940s, accessed
29 January 2025

103 Diana Nyad Official Website, https://diananyad.com,
accessed 27 October 2024

104 D Nyad, 'Nyad's journey: Never, ever give up' (2013),
www.youtube.com/watch?v=Zx8uYIfUvh4, accessed
27 October 2024

105 The Cuba Swim, Diana Nyad Official Website, https://
diananyad.com/the-cuba-swim, accessed 27 October 2024

106 *Nyad* (Netflix, 2023)

107 D Nyad, interview on *The Ellen DeGeneres Show*, YouTube,
www.youtube.com/watch?v=kQJofJjSayg, accessed
27 October 2024

108 D Nyad, interview with Dr Sanjay Gupta, CNN,
www.youtube.com/watch?v=plu-4wTZqf4, accessed
27 October 2024

109 EverWalk, https://everwalk.com

110 *The Straits Times*, 'Australian vet Craig Challen praised
for key role in Thai cave rescue' (11 July 2018), www.
straitstimes.com/asia/se-asia/australian-vet-who-was-
part-of-thai-cave-rescue-team, accessed 27 October 2024

111 *The Swimmers*, directed by Sally El Hosaini (Netflix, 2022),
www.netflix.com

112 BBC News, 'Australian of the Year award given to Thai
cave rescuers' (25 January 2019), www.bbc.com/news/
world-australia-46998069, accessed 27 October 2024

113 R Harris, *The Art of Risk: What we can learn from the world's leading risk-takers* (Simon & Schuster, 2024)

114 Joseph Rowntree Foundation, 'UK poverty 2024' (23 January 2024), www.jrf.org.uk, accessed 16 January 2025

115 H Rowe, *Eliminating Poverty in Britain* (The History Press, 2023)

116 H Rowe, Book Reviews, www.helenroweuk.net/book-reviews, accessed 27 October 2024

117 H Rowe, Training Course: The Biology of Poverty, www.helenroweuk.net, accessed 16 January 2025

118 *Robin Williams: Come inside my mind*, directed by Marina Zenovich (HBO, 2018), www.youtube.com/watch?v=FBg0d63ZHbk, accessed 27 October 2024

119 R Holiday, S Hanselman, *The Daily Stoic: 366 meditations on wisdom, perseverance, and the art of living* (Portfolio, 2016)

120 RK Greenleaf, *Servant Leadership*

121 D Markova, *I Will Not Die an Unlived Life: Reclaiming purpose and passion* (Red Wheel, 2000)

122 M Graham, *Blood Memory: An Autobiography* (Doubleday, 1991)

123 Presencing Institute (@presencing), 'Learn to lead from the emerging future…' Instagram (27 August 2024), www.instagram.com/presencing/reel/C_LlVrZAn-3/?hl=en, accessed 27 October 2024

124 R Arzón, *Shut Up and Run: How to get up, lace up, and sweat with swagger* (Harvest, 2024)

Acknowledgements

A s life grows more complex, some things become harder to navigate, and writing my second book was one. I am profoundly grateful to those who supported me in persisting through each stage, enabling me to shape what truly matters to me: distilling my core insights and passions into these pages, with the hope of sparking bold conversations that inspire even bolder change. Even if your name is not mentioned, please know you are deeply held in my heart with immense gratitude.

To my family – my husband Predrag and my son Noa – thank you for your unceasing support and for allowing my frequent physical and occasional mental absences from our sacred circle. Your commitment to my pace, even when it challenges us all, is a gift beyond measure.

To my parents – Jelena and Klaudio – thank you for your unshakeable belief in me that never stops.

To my book mentor, Karen Williams, my constant guide on this journey, who has graciously welcomed my thoughts, whether coherent or otherwise, on to paper. Your compassion, passion and authenticity in our conversations have been invaluable. Thank you, Karen, for nurturing my growth as an author and as an authority in the field of bold leadership.

To my Co-Active coach, Ronnie Clifford, for our years of brilliant conversation and for that unforgettable moment of grabbing me by the throat at the height of our coaching session to spark my immediate growth. You are a master coach for a reason. I am honoured our paths have crossed. When I grow up, I want to be you.

To my friend and kindred spirit, Mirjam Johansson, who, for the second time, has helped me better understand my own writing. You are far more than my 'biggest fan', as you say; you are my teacher. I only hope I can one day return half the gold you've given me when your own books are ready to be shared. Hurry, we need your words.

To my other wonderful friends who helped me clarify my ideas: Günter Westphal, Vinay Kumar, Art

Blanchford, Tiago Valentim, Xavier Garcia-Weibel and Jenny Leclezio. In times when time itself is scarce, you still found moments to connect and offer your best. I am deeply grateful for each of you.

To the entire Leadership Circle® – Bob Anderson, Bill and Cindy Adams, Carolina Páez Galvis, Jose Manuel Gil Gonzalez, and many more not mentioned but warmly remembered – thank you for your legacy, for supporting me as I build on it with my own, and for your friendship.

I am especially grateful to Bob – thank you for profoundly touching my journey through your trust in my writing. Your wholehearted and generous praise for this book moved me beyond what words can express.

To the unforgettable Liberto Pereda, who deepened my love for the Universal Model of Leadership. Though we've lost you in physical form, your spirit endures. To your son, Mario Pereda, whose masterful illustrations have empowered my words – thank you, Mario, for a wonderful partnership.

To the extraordinary leaders on the edge, Mel Young and Helen Rowe, who generously shared their stories with me, enriching both my soul and the words I've written here. I am deeply grateful. I cannot thank you enough.

The Homeless World Cup holds a special place in my heart and in this book. My interview with co-founder Mel highlights his extraordinary vision and dedication, providing an incredible example of leadership on the edge – bold, transformative and deeply impactful. To explore how you can support his mission, visit: https:// homelessworldcup.gofundraise.co.uk/cms/donate

Finally, to my wonderful clients, particularly Ana Gongola, Bruno Casadinho and Shail Jain, and to the many others not mentioned but thought of—you see me as your inspiration, but truly, you are mine. Without your stories, your trust, your boldness and your leaps into the unknown before my eyes, I would have no inspiration to share.

The Author

Zana Goic Petricevic is a leadership transformation expert, bold leadership coach for C-suite leaders, speaker and best-selling author of *Bold Reinvented: Next level leading with courage, consciousness, and conviction*, helping organisations to embrace change, adopt a bold mindset and take decisive risks to thrive. Zana's mission is to empower leaders to lead on the edge, pushing the boundaries of what's possible and creating impactful change.

With a university degree in languages and a master's degree in economics, Zana transitioned from a dynamic career in corporate communications and marketing within the oil and gas and pharmaceutical industries to focus on leadership development. She now inspires organisations across the globe with her compelling talks and cutting-edge leadership programmes.

As the founder of Bold Leadership Culture, a boutique leadership development consultancy based in Croatia and the UK with a global presence across the EU, USA and APAC, Zana is a recognised expert in coaching and leadership development. Her SOUL Framework®, featured in *Bold Reinvented*, forms the foundation of her company's global offerings, transforming how leaders engage with courage, consciousness and conviction.

Zana has coached and trained hundreds of leaders, partnering with global giants in diverse industries, including big tech, banking, pharmaceuticals, the Big Four, engineering and more. Her impressive client list includes PwC, Capgemini, UniCredit Bank, TikTok, Amazon, Sandoz and EU institutions, among others.

Living in Zagreb, Croatia, with her husband and son, Zana travels the world pursuing her passion – transforming leadership on a global scale.

Learn more at:

⊕ www.boldleadership-culture.com

⊕ www.zanagoicpetricevic.com

in www.linkedin.com/in/zanagoicpetricevic